OUTRAGED OF TUNBRIDGE WELLS

Original Letters
from
Middle England

Edited by
Nigel Cawthorne
with
Colin Cawthorne

GIBSON SQUARE

This edition first published in 2020 by Gibson Square.

ISBN: 9781783342013
email: rights@gibsonsquare.com
website: www.gibsonsquare.com

Papers used by Gibson Square are natural, recyclable products made from wood grown in sustainable forests; inks used are vegetable based. Manufacturing conforms to ISO 14001, and is accredited to FSC and PEFC chain of custody schemes. Colour-printing is through a certified CarbonNeutral® company that offsets its CO2 emissions.

Printed by CPI Group (UK) Ltd, Croydon CR0 4YY

CONTENTS

INTRODUCTION

There is a figure in the English language known simply as 'Disgusted of Tunbridge Wells' from the signature on the irate letter of complaint he – though frequently also, she – sent to the local newspapers in his town. While the precise historical origins of the phrase are of no fixed abode, the soubriquet conjures up an ex-Indian Army colonel who had retired to the spa town only to spend his last days railing anonymously against everything that is wrong with the Old Country and Modern Times.

As one of the letter writers below observes, to complain in public is a national birth-right: 'may I avail myself of the Britisher's privilege'. Just imagine what joy these small-town 'Britishers' would have squeezed from social media. Online they could furtively have pelted Britain with their spleen, unfiltered by pesky editors. On Twitter and elsewhere no one in Britain or, indeed, the world would be safe from their withering opinions. Coalescing in eddies of discontent, they would egg each other on. The secret, perenially-upset cohorts from Tunbridge Wells were well ahead of their time without knowing it.

But they weren't just disgusted in Tunbridge Wells.

They were also peeved, niggled, indignant, acrimonious, belligerent and, more often than not, outraged. And, without having the benefit of the internet, once they gave vent to their feelings of disapprobation in the letters pages of the now, sadly, long defunct *Tunbridge Wells Advertiser.**

The authors of these letters appear to have walked in directly from the pages of Agatha Christie – or even P.G. Wodehouse. For all their petty concerns, they hailed from a literate age. Their letters are no blathering, repetitive rants. They are sometimes larded with Biblical and classical references, though most carry their learning lightly. And they are funny – some deliberately so, but more often because the subject does not quite warrant the intensity of aggravation that is expressed. Then there are letters that are purposefully provocative, aimed to inflame and bait the other correspondents. The end result is invariably an explosion of outrage.

As the other pages of the *Tunbridge Wells Advertiser* (incorporating the *Sevenoaks & Tonbridge Observer, & Kent & Sussex Herald*, the masthead says) were full of 'fashionable marriages', adverts for stays and gentlemen playing tennis wearing long trousers and blazers, it would be tempting to imagine that 'Outraged of Tunbridge Wells' is long gone. True, ex-Colonels returning from running the rajah are now nursing their whisky-and-sodas in a saloon bar in the sky and succeeding generations of newspaper editors have learnt to be more guarded when parading prejudices. But in the heyday of the *Tunbridge Wells Advertiser* there were no such inhibitions, so what we read in the letters page is the authentic voice of middle England, a masterclass in the proper English way of airing a complaint.

There are enduring irritants – late trains, extortionate taxi fares, youths misbehaving on buses, rudeness on the telephone, the lack of discipline and moral fibre. The answer to these problems is corporal punishment and temperance, it seems.

Carol singers are a nuisance and wine should not be served with Christmas lunch. Then there are the Mormons who are coming to take our women, the ever-present danger posed by the Church of Rome, fast cars, appalling things on the radio, cinema and television, people singing, dancing and playing sports on a Sunday, mixed bathing and women – 'female relatives, friends or fancy bits' – who are allowed to don the hallowed uniform of the Home Guard.

There is a letter from the Fascist Club for Children in Nevill Street that teaches youngsters to love God and honour the King, and holds back the 'Red Revolution' – which it is hard to imagine was much of a threat in Tunbridge Wells. The unemployed should be put to work building a seawall – in Tunbridge Wells? – meanwhile the clients of jobbing gardeners are too mean to pay them for clearing snow from clients' drives and doorsteps.

One temperance advocate wrote to inform the *Advertiser*'s readership that General Lord Napier's men scaled the mountains of Abyssinia and took Magdala without a single drop of strong liquor. Three sailors wrote in because they heard that the girls from Tunbridge Wells were the best in Britain, and were overwhelmed with replies. There is the correspondent who withholds his name and condemns the *Advertiser*'s editor as a 'war crank' because the paper reports the slaughter of the First World War. Although it was not the paper's policy to print anonymous letters, the editor made an exception in that case – good on him, 'Outraged of Tunbridge' would say. But should music by German composers really be played during the war? And what was the cause of the Second World War?

What's more it's an outrage in a Christian country that Tunbridge Wells' North Ward should elect as councillors a brewer and a 'pleasure-monger' – that is, the director of the local opera house. On a lighter note, a chicken laid a six-inch egg with three yolks. But surely people who allow their cocks to crow in the morning should be arrested for disturbing the peace, not to mention the flood of itinerant organ-grinders who engulfed the town.

But perhaps most appealing of all is Mr E.R. Drake who uses the letters page to tell the good people of Tunbridge Wells that their town is 'full of old maids, pet dogs and parsons' and is '200 years behind the times'.

My son and I combed through the yellowing pages of the *Tunbridge Wells Advertiser* back to the beginning of the last century. Every day at lunch and in the evening we swapped tales of the gems were had unearthed. I hope you get as much pleasure from these scenes of a time gone by and expositions of well-mannered spleen-venting as we did. Long may there be outrage in Britain.

Town Slackers

Taxes and death are unavoidable – fine. But surely that means that, at the very least, the tax payer should get his money's worth for public services rendered? So why does everything have to be so slack, so slow, so useless, so pointless, once the town government spends our money?

VISITORS' RELIEF

SIR – Quite recently I paid a visit to Tunbridge Wells, and noticed with pleasure the many vast improvements made in the town, and having spent my younger days in the neighbourhood I naturally have quite a *penchant* for the place.

There is one thing, however, lacking, which I consider of utmost importance, and which, I think, should have special attention, viz.: the establishment of conveniences for ladies and gentlemen. There is not one public place in the town. Surely this is an oversight. In every well-organised resort one finds this convenience. I queried a constable, but he gave me the negative. I think the local government of Tunbridge Wells should give this their attention forthwith.

JOHN T. CLARIDGE

April 24th, 1903

PUBLIC INCONVENIENCES

SIR – I always thought we had a body of gentlemen on our Council who devoted their time to improvement and also to promote attractions for visitors. But, comparing the advantages of Tunbridge Wells with Eastbourne, I find the former considerably behind the latter.

From the Redoubt in the east of Eastbourne to Beachy Head in the west, at about equal distances, you will find lavatories on the most improved principles both for ladies and gentlemen. I believe there is one for ladies here [in Tunbridge Wells] at the

Baths in Monson Road, out of sight for any visitor. I understand that tradesmen are often put to inconvenience in this matter of the ladies.

Our seats – I am informed that there are about 180 on the two Commons. As I am constantly over and around both, I can truly say that quite half are only fit to chop up and burn out of the way. Again, if you take a walk anywhere in Eastbourne with a radius of a mile, you will find seats to seat five people, well-made, newly painted, and kept clean.

What do you find here? A miserable two on the Forest Road, where hundreds of persons are continually going to our Cemetery. All around the rest of the outskirts, if you want to rest, you have to do so on your umbrella or on the wet ground.

On the seashore you can have a deckchair with hood for 2d. for the whole morning, afternoon or evening.

Other matters I could mention, but must forbear.

ONE WHO IS NOT USUALLY A GRUMBLER
August 9th, 1912

UNLADY-LIKE

SIR – I was spending an afternoon in your town last week, and, being a stranger, made inquiries for the ladies' lavatory, and to my surprise I was told there were none nearer than the station. I should have thought in a town like this there would be no less than three lavatories for ladies. I noticed several for men, but it seems that the things of

11

greatest importance are left out in your beautiful town...

LIZZIE

February 21st, 1913

RASPBERRY

SIR – Some time ago I read in your valuable paper of the great profit which some Town Councillor claimed would be derived from the cultivation of logan berries on the Sewage Farms, and that the Tunbridge Wells Town Council had decided to invest in some plants, with the view of the reduction of our rates. Can you say how much profit has been the result of the enterprise, and was the flavour satisfactory?

RATEPAYER

November 11th, 1910

CROSS PURPOSED

SIR – It is unfortunate that the first timorous effort on the part of the Town authorities to extend the pleasurable use of our splendid swimming baths should be marred by such unfavourable weather... however, other reasons will prevent the success of the scheme...The regulations were framed, I am given to understand, with the object of allowing 'Family', but preventing 'Mixed' bathing, but all they succeed in doing is to prevent all but a fortunate few from enjoying the privilege. They obviously do not succeed in carrying out their intentions. If I take my sister to

12

the baths, and my friend takes his, I presume we 'Family bathe', but if I take his and he takes mine, I understand we 'Mix.' Now once in the water, where is the difference?

P.R. SMITH
Queen's Road
August 30th, 1912

BROWN BATHS

SIR – My club, having been mainly instrumental in procuring permission from the Council for the Baths to be used at certain times for mixed bathing, I am desired on their behalf to express a hope that the people of Tonbridge will take advantage of this useful innovation.

As there appears to be a wrong idea amongst a few people as to the freshness of the water, I should like to point out that the Bath is emptied entirely twice a week and partly every day. This stands in favourable comparison with any other public swimming baths, as very few are emptied oftener. The reason of the water appearing discoloured is owing to it consisting partly of river water (filtered), and also because the bottom of the bath is concrete and not tiles, of which the bottoms of most baths are composed.

ROGER W. LEONARD
Hon. Sec. Tonbridge Swimming Club
June 13th, 1913

TARRED AND BRUSHED

SIR – Why has the open-air bath been tarred? Was it to keep the dust down or the bathers? It is having the double effect, and there are some wonderful studies in black and white emerging from the discoloured water, after which paraffin is in great demand from the obliging attendant.

A BATHER

July 20th, 1923

SHOCKING STANDARDS

SIR – As I was passing over the Grosvenor-bridge on Wednesday, I saw a most distressing accident. A horse in a heavy coal van had fallen down, and becoming entangled in the harness and shafts, struggled in vain to rise.

The driver (a lad) and others appealed to three or four of the Corporation men who were repairing the pavement not ten yards away, for assistance, and, would you believe it, not one of them would move an inch, but stood there with their mouths wide open looking on. Thanks to Mr Roberts, veterinary surgeon, and others who came up afterwards, the horse escaped with a few nasty cuts.

Now, Sir as one who has watched the movements of the Corporation men for years, and has seen the regular pace (about two miles an hour) when moving from one part of the town to another, surely they could spare five minutes in a case like that?

HUMANITY

June 28th, 1901

DISGUSTING POST

SIR – To inaugurate the birth of the 20th Century we in Southborough are getting our early morning letters with our lunch. Thus, thanks to the superior intelligence of the postal authorities at Tunbridge Wells.

Sometime during the last year the Tunbridge Wells authorities began making enquires as to the volume of the Post Office trade done in Southborough. These enquiries seem to have been made at what was a comparatively slack time in the local offices, and it is on the returns then obtained that the present changes have been made. These alterations, briefly, consist in changing the whole of the postmen over to different rounds, putting a lot of extra work and worry on their shoulders, and the result is – infinite annoyance to the community because of the lateness of deliveries.

As an example of what is now taking place I may mention that this (Wednesday) morning it was after half-past nine before one of the postmen got out with his letters, and this man happens to have to serve one of the largest and most important rounds in the neighbourhood. He should have finished his early morning work within five minutes of the time when he started out on his round!

Perhaps the worst piece of business in the whole re-arrangement of matters is the treatment which has been meted out to the old mail cart driver Thrift. I hold no brief for, nor am I acquainted with him,

15

but, nevertheless, I feel that the way in which he has been treated is nothing short of scandalous. I am told that for 27 years or thereabouts he has driven the mail cart between Tunbridge Wells and Southborough, and now, after serving the best years of his life at this special work, the postal authorities at Tunbridge Wells have discovered that he is unfit for these duties – that he is too work-worn to carry on the mail work – and therefore, in order to provide for his declining years, have set him the task of walking some ten miles a day delivering letters!

Surely in the interests of justice sufficient pressure will be brought to bear upon the Tunbridge Wells Postmaster to at any rate rectify this matter (even if we have to put up with the late delivery) and it is with the object of seeing what your other readers think that I am writing you.

DISGUSTED

January 2nd 1901

CROSSED WIRES

SIR – Referring to the circular sent by the Borough of Tunbridge Wells to the citizens, giving terms upon which they propose to start a Municipal Telephone Service, would it not be as well to bear in mind that:

1st – As yet the Borough possesses no licence from the General Post Office.

2nd – Subscribers to the proposed Municipal Service would not be able to communicate with subscribers to the National Telephone Company, thus requiring uses to have two sets of instruments –

and the greatest nuisance of all two directories to refer to when in want of a subscribers number.

3rd – And also to many a very important matter, that the Borough requires a pre-payment of two pounds, ten shillings, whereas the existing Telephone Company require no cash in advance, merely a guarantee of sending so many messages per month – and by the party line system a subscriber can send two messages per month and receive an unlimited number of messages for £3 per annum; and a very different amount to the £5 17s 6d quoted in the Municipal circular.

> Yours truly
> **KNOWLES**
> January 15th, 1900

WASTING OUR TIME AND MONEY

SIR – 'Please ignore this application if payment has been made during the three days prior to the date shown above.' No, I won't ignore it. I will give it as much publicity as possible. The above is the wording of a South Eastern Electricity Board final notice for a quarterly electricity account, sent out about a month after the original bill. Of course, by the time I received the final notice I had paid the account – two days before. How long does it take for a local office to notify the central accounts office at Eastbourne that a customer has paid up?

Isn't this wasted manpower (and postage) typical of the clogged wheels of bureaucracy that we suffer today? Is it surprising that we cannot find time (out of our own working time) to pay electricity accounts when the local office shuts for the lunch-hour and at 5 p.m.?

Incidentally, telephones head office also does its best to discourage people from paying their accounts. It shuts at 4 p.m.

WORKER

November 24th, 1954

GETTING AWAY WITH IT

SIR – The disastrous farm fire at Pembury last week was caused according to report, by a spark from a lorry engine. If this is a fact, it shows how many fires may occur during the next few weeks owning to drought. I understand there is a law prohibiting smoke issuing from engines on the highway. If this is a fact, why do the police allow it? I saw one go through Church Road recently pouring out its blackening smoke all over the place. Is it allowed, if not, why is it not stopped?

RATEPAYER

August 30th, 1935

APPALLING LACK OF STICK

SIR – What is the use of an Anti-Socialist Committee whose activities appear to be limited to opposing independent non-Socialists and attempting to make working arrangements with strong Socialist candidates?

I suggest that the next time the occasion arises

18

for a presentation in recognition of services to be made to an official of the local Anti-Socialist Committee, it should take the form of a big stick (suitably draped with Union Jack) and a box of eggs (preferably imported from Russia). Then what valiant deeds we should see.

L.W. PASSMORE

October 9th, 1928

INCOMPETENT FAT CATS

SIR – May I ask for space for the following: –

I am an owner and occupier of property in Tunbridge Wells, and have been on the register as a Parliamentary voter for 19 years, and now (as I understand) through the carelessness of officials in crossing my name off the register instead of another person's I have lost my vote at this Election.

I, for one, think it quite time that these highly-paid officials should be held responsible in a monetary sense for the careless way in which they do their duties, and from which there appears to be no redress at the time.

TAXED BUT NOT REPRESENTED

January 19th, 1906

Infernal Roads

*Tunbridge Wells is heaven on earth, but at least the
road to hell is apparently properly paved and easy to
walk on. Can anyone explain why it is impossible to
go from A to B in this town without killing one's self
in the process? Does the town Corporation bear a
secret death-wish towards those who pay its wages?*

MUD ON THE PAVEMENTS

SIR – The condition of the road and footpath leading from Southborough Station to Upper Grosvenor Road has been for years, during the winter months especially, a disgrace to the town and to civilisation.

It has at times, in fact during the last few months, been well nigh impossible for pedestrians to pass backwards and forwards to the station of High Brooms with any comfort, and it is extremely unpleasant, not to say dangerous, to start for a railway journey with one's feet smothered in mire.

I am aware that building operations have a good deal to do with the state of the road, as well as the heavy traffic from the brickworks etc., but this is no excuse for the evident neglect for the road, and especially of the footpath by the responsible authorities.

Complaints have been frequent and certainly not without reason, and sincerely trust that the footpath especially will be at once properly made up, and the road put in order, particularly at the crossing from the path to the station entrance, where the mud accumulates to a surprising extent.

I would also draw attention to the broken posts of the galvanized iron fence by the side of the path, which are extremely dangerous and might easily cause serious accident, especially at night.

JOSEPH J. GREEN
March 5th, 1901

21

TAR IDIOTS

SIR – When all the town of Tunbridge Wells has been trying this week to make the place agreeable to the visitors – how do you think the South Eastern Railway Company did their part?

Why, by having the paths around their station covered with fresh liquid tar.

A VISITOR

July 15th, 1904

ROAD RIGHTS

SIR – Will you allow me a small space in your valuable paper to call the attention of the Borough Council to the bad state of the cinder path in Camden Park; the last few weeks it has been in a very muddy state. Last Monday a motor car travelled on the path through the park, driving foot-passengers off the pathway, and to-day a horse and cart has gone through on the path. With the large number of people who use this path, I think, as a ratepayer for nearly 30 years, something should be done to stop this nuisance.

Yours faithfully,

PEDESTRIAN.

February 16th, 1906

SWEPT TO EXTREMES

SIR – As a resident householder of some six years' standing, I desire to bear my testimony to the benefits of the salubrious air and the beautiful surroundings of Tunbridge Wells and its Commons. But, sir, I and many others, have a grievance, or rather two, and I should like to make them known to you.

I reside at the further end of the Upper Grosvenor Road, and to reach the Common or the town have a good twenty minutes' walk. At the time I leave home for my mornings walk, say, 10 to 10.30 a.m. (generally accompanied by my wife), about three times a week, we have to pass through a cloud of dust, caused by the sweepers – about eight in number – and breathe the countless microbes raised by them, and floating in the air; and on our return, say, 1 to 1.30 p.m., generally have to pass through the same ordeal for our road is a long one.

I know it is necessary for the road to be swept, and I must admit it is kept in beautiful order, but could it not be done before 10 a.m., say, by doubling the number of sweepers and having the time, or otherwise?

The second grievance is the refuse and dust carts! They commence their journeys between 5.30 and 6 a.m., disturbing and shaking those who do not or cannot rise so early, and more or less are passing, full or empty, until 6.30 p.m. Morning, noon, and evening we meet these lumbering, noisy, objectionable refuse dust carts!

Sir cannot this state of affairs be remedied? Is there no way out of this nuisance, no other route? Would not a refuse destructor, the same as in other towns, meet the difficulty, and by utilising the refuse, cause a saving in the rates?

I am sure the residents, from the Grosvenor

Bridge onwards, would bear me out in my statement, and I had not the slightest idea when I took my house for a term of years that I should be subjected to such an intolerable nuisance.

We know what King Solomon said about the dead flies in the pot of ointment, but thank goodness, the evils that I complain of can be removed by a little foresight and care on the part of the authorities, and I hope the day will soon come when I shall be able to sign myself.

ANTI-GRUMBLER

July 26th, 1907

MILKED OFF

SIR – In the last issue of this paper a correspondent complained about the noise made by thoughtless milkmen (and others) in the early hours of the mornings. It is not by their own wish that they are about at such UNEARTHLY hours. Maybe that correspondent would care to change places with them.

We wonder if your readers would care to advocate a law that no person should start work before eight o'clock? Then your correspondent would have cause to grouse if the milk was not delivered before five minutes past eight.

Perhaps your correspondent also likes to have two deliveries of milk on Sunday, and never so much as a 'please' or 'thank you.' Then they sit in chapel and think how good they are to their fellow-brethren.

EIGHT NOISY MILKMEN

February 26th, 1927

POTENTIAL DEATH TRAPS

SIR – Here is another 'grouse' from the East Ward. The pavement outside St. James's Schools (Quarry Road side) is in a disgraceful condition; the surface is very uneven and rough. This is very dangerous for children attending the school, especially the infants. Boys will be boys, and girls will be girls, and tumbles are frequent. Surely the authorities can make a good job of this by laying a proper pavement, before some serious accident occurs? Perhaps the Councillors who represent us on the Council have walked on the other side of the road, and failed to notice this. However, perhaps the 'powers that be' will wake up and do something.

ANOTHER GROUSER.

March 24th, 1939

ANKLE TWITCHING

SIR – On many occasions I have called attention to the brick paving in Tunbridge Wells. Many of the residents are aged, and perhaps infirm, having had to retire through ill-health, and have come to Tunbridge Wells on the advice of their doctor!

What do they find? That many of the streets are steep, and paved with uneven bricks. Take, for instance, Mount Pleasant, Molyneux Park and adjacent roads, Mount Ephraim, the Pantiles, etc. These make one's legs tired, and their ankles swell.

I often notice people's ankles those who suffer

from bad feet and swollen ankles in this town seem to outnumber the people similarly afflicted in other non-brick towns.

ANKLEITIS

August 19th, 1938

BRUISING POST

SIR – If no useful purpose is served by the small post on the pavement near the junction of High Street and Castle Street, why isn't it uprooted before some unfortunate pedestrian meets with serious injury as a result of its dangerous presence? I was almost the victim of such injury few nights ago, and it was only because the excessive darkness necessitated very slow progress that I escaped with nothing worse than a bad bruise.

Maybe the post referred to has some use that is not apparent to the uninitiated. If that is so, immediate steps should be taken to make it as visible as possible during darkness. White paint or reflecting studs would help a lot, and as I suspect many others besides myself have been caught in the trap, the danger of the obstruction would be lessened.

A VICTIM

November 7th, 1941

TERRIFYING JOLTS

SIR – The main road between Sevenoaks and Tunbridge Wells is sown with sunken manhole covers and hydrant inspection lids; occasionally for a change of hazard they stick up above the surface, so that the riders of light motor-cycles and motorized bicycles are constantly falling into pits or bumping into obstacles.

During daylight they can often be avoided, though not in traffic, but at night every rider of these machines must have had dozens of terrifying jolts in the darkness.

After some months as a motor scooterist, I know most of the worst ones and very sudden and frightening their impact can be. I should like to protest very warmly at these unnecessary dangers and I hope others will support me.

> **WASP**
>
> October 7th, 1953

WHO RUNS OUR TOWN?

SIR – What is wrong with our Town Council? When someone else is going to foot the bill for repairs to the High Street it seems ridiculous to me that they can't do the job properly. I read with astonishment that after nearly £11,000 has been spent, the High Street will still have a two feet drop from one side to the other. Our only consolation is that the slope will be levelled out. It appears that the council is afraid of displeasing the tradesmen in that part of the town. Who are these shopkeepers that the public have to suffer because they are afraid that customers will dislike extra steps to the pavement?

Do they run this town or do we, the majority of private householders? As a motorist who constantly

27

makes use of the High Street, I regard their narrow minded, selfish attitude as a stumbling block to progress in Tunbridge Wells. Ask the average man in the street what he would prefer – a level road or a one-in-eight tilt?

        J.K.N.

July 21st, 1954

SHOPPING MAYHEM

SIR – Who was responsible for leaving that muddy extraction on Saturday last week in the narrow pavement on the corner of Grosvenor Road and Goods Station Road? Were the so-called public services to blame? Would it not have been possible for the workmen concerned to have put in an extra hour tidying up the site and leaving the footway unobstructed and clean?

No! One can just imagine them downing tools 'on the dot' on Saturday morning without a thought to the Saturday shopping crowds.

What did the boss of the job order? Who, in short, is the anonymous somebody who was cursed so thoroughly by hundreds of shoppers on Saturday?

One hopes that his wife was one of the scores who suffered not merely the inconvenience of dirt but the actual danger of pushing a pram into the road – and one hopes that she let her selfish unimaginative husband know what was thought of the mess he left.

        JUST A SHOPPER

October 28th, 1953

Pesky Noises

Tunbridge Wells is Britain's Garden of Eden. But, I ask you, was the Garden of Eden ever terrorised by noise produced at considerable volume by inconsiderate neighbours? Case closed.

CLOCKWORK RAGE

SIR – Of what use is the striking of clocks in our town?

I live under the shadow of St. John's and the clock during the night is a considerable annoyance to me and my household. In case of illness it might be a serious check to recovery. I believe that if a plebiscite were taken from the residents within a radius of (say) a quarter of a mile from the church, there would be a large majority in favour of silence – especially during the night.

The striking of public clocks comes from a time when clocks and watches were more expensive, and therefore scarcer than at present. There can be very few houses in the town with no time recorder.

There appears to me to be no public advantage in the practice, more especially when the clocks, as is often the case, are not in agreement, and flaunt their difference in the night air.

GLEN

March 16th 1926

ALIEN ATTACK

SIR – Surely something ought to be done to at least mitigate the organ-grinding nuisance, which appears to have become an institution in our midst.

As I write (Saturday morning) the 'Holy City' is being murdered by the double instrument (of torture) of barrel organ and cornet, and at quite a late hour last night we had the same infliction with a crescendo on the cornet, the result making the night hideous.

It is impossible to conceive of any other motives than boredom for giving pecuniary help to such really impudent aliens who are not content with a refusal at the door, but trample on the flower bed to attract my attention by staring and shouting at me through the window, and this too, after giving personal instruction not to call again.

In some towns this class of mendicant is rigidly excluded; action of this sort will be imposed upon us if we are to attract those in search of rest and quiet. Thanking you in advance.

W. H. GRIFFIN.

September 5th, 1902

BUGLING BLIGHT

SIR – The evening bugle practice close to the residential part of the Common wakes all the babies and young children in the neighbourhood, and constitutes a nuisance, which, if not discontinued, will speedily cause visitors with young families to leave the town, and will also prevent others similarly situated from visiting it.

A VISITOR

May 15th, 1903

NO UNCERTAIN TONE

SIR – As a resident of some years I should like to protest against the rapidly increasing number of street musicians, who, while apparently making a

31

good living here, are damaging the reputation of Tunbridge Wells. In the road in which I live we suffer from seven different sets of musical (?) performers, not including the various organ grinders. I am doing what little I can to mitigate this appalling nuisance. Will not other householders do likewise?

RATEPAYER

April 7th, 1905

HAIR-RAISING ENGINES

SIR – As a lover of music, I am impelled to make a protest with reference to the increased 'bedlam' at the band performances, caused in its near and immediate vicinity by some people who bring dogs; and also the 'hair-raising' noises of motorists, who make a garage of the lower road at the back of the Pantiles. They come and listen to the music for nothing for a time, then 'konk' up their engines regardless of the comfort and feelings of others 'in the pictures.'

Surely this is a slur on the great art, which is worthy of far greater consideration?

I noticed with much satisfaction that Mr P.F. Battishill one morning last week stopped his band in the middle of a piece on account of the disturbances caused by a dog, and resumed playing after it was removed.

Such measures are stern, but necessary, in order to prevent this thoughtlessness.

A RESIDENT

August 31st, 1923

32

DOWN-AND-OUT BANDS

SIR – Following your Current Comment on Itinerant Bands last week cannot something be done to prevent these unwanted people from invading our beautiful town? Surely the Watch Committee though the Chief Constable can secure powers to prevent a repetition of the undignified scenes which occurred last Thursday. Such scenes as were witnessed in Mount Pleasant would not be tolerated in any other town of the class of Tunbridge Wells.

'DISGUSTED'

April 17th, 1931

LOUD-SPEAKING DEATH-TRAPS

SIR – No doubt it is necessary, for success in business, to advertise freely, but is there no limit to the annoyances which the public may be subjected to by advertisers? Two or three days ago a large van was going though Tunbridge Wells advertising gramophone records by means of loudspeakers on the van roof. Apart from the nuisance caused to householders and others, it appears to be that this practice is extremely dangerous, both to pedestrians and to drivers of motor vehicles by distracting their attention when they are on the roads. I would suggest that the Town Council should make a bye-law prohibiting this practice.

ANTI-NOISE

May 4th, 1934

33

Disgusting Dogs

Dogs are man's best friend. So, too, in Tunbridge Wells and dogs are bathed in much affection. But some take exception – cat lovers for example – and others incline towards a more neutral position: the one holding the firm truncheon of the law...

DOG TOILETS

SIR – Whilst it is interesting to note that the national anti-litter campaign is having a certain amount of effect, one cannot help thinking that Tunbridge Wells would benefit by a campaign against a rather obnoxious problem – that of 'Dog Nuisance.' This somewhat difficult problem at times reaches the point of being, if not a danger to health, a source of potential physical danger to the unwary pedestrian.

The part of Tunbridge Wells in which I live appears to be particularly prone to this form of nuisance, and the point which never ceases to amaze me is the complete lack of sense of guilt exhibited by the human being whom the offending animals take out for walks. The other evening I was forced to leap like a young gazelle over an out-stretched lead rather than wait possibly for some minutes for a dog to take the fullest advantage of my drive. The human at the other end of the lead did not attempt to move and remained completely unshaken by both my glare and my minor display of athletics.

I would not wish to be drawn into a discussion on the relative rights and wrongs of keeping domestic pets, although if the happiness of the animal is reflected in the faces of their lead-holder-owners, then I feel rather sorry for some of them. However, in these enlightened times there should be some practical solution which could be found to suit both dog owners and dogless alike.

One solution which immediately springs to my

mind is the provision of modified dog conveniences of a very simple construction – possibly in
the form of 'walks,' which could be subjected to
chemical purifying action – placed at strategic
positions. But please let it be at the expense of the
dog owner and not at the expense of the already
over-burdened ratepayer. Surely part of the annual
licence fee could be annexed for this purpose or a
small addition made to the licence fee for this
specific purpose? Unless some practical solution is
demanded, it seems that there will never be an end
to this objectionable problem.

T. JAMES

September 15th, 1954

INTOLERABLE CANINE INQUISITION

SIR – English ladies and gentlemen who have gone
to Ireland, or abroad, taking their dogs with them,
find themselves on their return subjected to
systematic persecution, inexcusable and intolerable
to the last degree. A large number of cases of such
hardship and unwarrantable interference with their
private property, their dogs, have been brought to
the notice of the National Canine Defence League;
and in all a bitter cry has been raised of the insolent
tyranny, despotic cruelty, shameful persecution, red
tape calumny, trouble and needless expense, etc.,
etc. Perfectly healthy dogs taken from England
brought back still in the same healthy condition,
even from Ireland and Norway, where rabies is said
to be unknown, are pursed with a more-than-

36

Corsican-vengeance by the British Board of Agriculture: such a state of affairs should no longer be permitted to disgrace England.

C.A.M. BAILEY

July 9th, 1900

BRAINLESS GAWPERS

SIR – I was delighted to see a letter and your comments in your paper today on dog variety, and hope your readers will do as I do, abstain from patronising any and every variety show whereof an item is the unnatural antics of any dogs.

I cannot imagine how anybody but a brainless idiot could possibly find pleasure in witnessing the like, and hope that Tunbridge Wells will show its sense of duty towards quadrupeds as well as make some show of braininess by making as decided a stand against the performance of four-footers in its Opera House during the variety season as my friend, Mr Stather Hunt, does against the use of incense and vestments in his Church.

HENRY JAMES ST BENNO CULIFFE (M.A. Oxon)

20, Eaton-gardens

July 5th, 1912

DOG VARIETY

SIR – As a society established for the protection of dogs from suffering, we have been urged by many lovers of animals to enter a protest against performances given by troupes of dogs in variety theatres.

C.R. JOHNS

National Canine Defence League

July 4th, 1912

CHAIN CHARITY

SIR – These are dry days – especially for dogs.

Although there is no prohibition against placing drinking-bowls outside doorways, we see very few now-a-days. Even shops which sell dog biscuits seem to have ceased to hold out the invitation, 'Drink, puppy, drink!'

We would like to see a return to the pre-war custom of 'free drinks for dogs,' but we suggest that the bowls be chained or firmly secured in other ways, as a precaution against theft.

CHARLES J. JOHNS

National Canine Defence League

July 16th, 1925

DOGS THAT PANT TOO MUCH

SIR – It has been brought to my notice that the old bad practice, so prevalent in the days before the motor car of making dogs run behind a bicycle, is once again being revived, and even in city streets one sees the unpleasant spectacle of panting, worried animals trying to keep up a speed beyond their strength.

One can easily imagine the agony of mind of the unhappy dog toiling in the wake of a vehicle with feverish anxiety lest he lose sight of his master in the busy traffic and straining every nerve to follow him. A correspondent tells me that he recently saw an aged spaniel so exhausted and so far behind his mounted owner that he could not keep a straight route but was following a zig-zag course among the cars and buses to his own danger and that of the drivers.

I would strongly urge dog owners to abstain from this cruel practice and either to cycle very slowly or else to exercise their animals on foot.

S. G. POLHILL

September 15th, 1944

VERMIN TERMINATION

SIR – I nearly didn't write on the subject of 'Dogs,' but after slipping on some filth on the path in Camden Road and falling to the ground my mind was made up.

It should be made an offence for any dog to be running the streets at any time. Numbers of half-starved and collarless dogs are a disgusting sight and a very bad moral influence on juveniles and a revolting sight to adults. I have seen people come into parks with a dog on a lead and immediately let it off the lead to relieve itself and then children run around and sit in some of this filth. Then what of the people who let their dogs foul the roads and paths and which the road sweepers have to sweep up? Let these people have the filth in their own gardens and clear up after their pets. A lady a few doors away from me slipped on some in Norman Road and broke her wrist and was attending the hospital for some weeks.

Last, but not least, what of the poor little cats?

Mine, for instance, has dogs each side that chase him, and if he goes over the gate he is also chased by dogs that way, and if the poor little cat sits in the front garden dogs are barking and tearing at the fence to get at him. Make it an offence for any dog to be about the streets, and if it has no collar and nameplate have it destroyed.

ANGRY AND DISGUSTED

October 7th, 1953

THIEVING CATS

SIR – It was not my intention to write about 'Cats,' but I cannot let 'Angry and Disgusted's' letter pass without comment.

I am extremely annoyed by this unjustified attack on dogs. Why should a dog, who is man's best friend, be a target for all this unjust criticism? How many accidents one wonders have been caused by cats? They are just as likely to cause a motorist to swerve, or a pedestrian to trip, as a dog, but we never hear about that.

The public are obliged to suffer the nuisance of other people's cats scratching up their gardens and allotments, quite apart from the unholy row which they kick up at all hours of the night by fighting and courting on other people's property. Most dogs sleep in at night, but cats – alas, no!

I am a lover of both, so fair play for all, please can 'Angry and Disgusted' honestly say that her 'Poor little cat' never leaves its own property to misbehave itself on someone else's?

In the past I have been obliged to keep my windows closed in order to keep other people's cats out. On two occasions I lost our luncheon fish which was left on the kitchen table, and the second time I actually caught somebody else's cat calmly eating it under the cooker.

Another time I returned home to find my dining-room literally covered with fur, and a battle royal still in progress. Needless to say, I had to clean up the mess.

Dogs may have their faults, but cats are no angels either. Equal rights and taxes for both, please.

INFURIATED TAIL-WAGGER

October 14th, 1953

REVOLTING DOGS

SIR – Would you kindly spare a little space in the 'Advertiser' to answer 'Infuriated Tailwagger.'

I would still like to see a better round-up by police of all stray dogs. Could and should a tax be made for cats, I would be willing to pay one for my cat. I should have the knowledge of having something for my money, meaning a 'Vermin Destroyer.'

I have never heard of a cat as being the cause of a serious accident. Also, has your correspondent ever seen six, seven or maybe more cats behaving disgustingly about the streets, as dogs do, which is a very common sight in Tunbridge Wells and as I have seen?

As for 'Serenades in the night,' we have on occasions a stray dog in the street below our window, barking and howling the whole night through.

I wouldn't go so far as to say my cat never leaves his own property but he doesn't get much chance around this way, for there are dogs, north, south, east and west, as well as the people who chase them. We have had the same trouble with doors and windows but usually with a little forethought it can be remedied. Re losing the luncheon fish, I would advise your correspondent to put it in a safe place, or run the risk of it being stolen by some poor half-starved cat.

And as for the Tunbridge Wells Council:– They barred the use of sale boards for empty houses, why not bar dogs from running the streets, which in my estimation is far more unsightly?

ANGRY AND DISGUSTED

October 28th, 1953

WHAT OF VILE CHILDREN?

SIR – It is beyond my comprehension why your correspondent should advocate the annihilation of all stray dogs, and yet appear to condone the misdeeds of cats (stray or otherwise), and appear to be under the impression that the other should get away with it.

I would be prepared to pay any tax, however high, to keep my dog, and still consider that I was getting more than my money's-worth. The dog is not only a faithful and devoted friend, but an excellent guard and defender of the home. It is also sufficiently intelligent to be trained to do almost anything, including the respect of roads and pavements. I am proud to say that my dog is sufficiently well-trained in obedience and cleanliness, to enable me to take it anywhere and everywhere without fear of embarrassment. As to the remark about their bad moral effect on children, there is not much it would seem that one can teach the modern child in that respect these days, they appear to be more well-informed than their parents.

I might also add that if I lost my fish through my own carelessness in leaving it where I was perfectly entitled to leave it with safety, a little more care and foresight could have prevented your correspondent's accident. The latter appears to be fully aware of the dangerous state of the pavements.

INFURIATED TAIL-WAGGER
November 4th, 1953

CAGE CLOSED

SIR – Having written to you last week criticising dogs – and their owners – I sat back awaiting outraged cries of protest. What happened? All I received were some very nice letters expressing agreement with what I had said.

Here are two typical examples. The first is from a Tunbridge Wells professional man. He says he favours 'the right dog in the right place at the right time,' and suggests that farmers' working dogs should continue to be exempt from tax. Another letter I had was from a Tunbridge Wells housewife. 'Raise the fee to £2,' she says. 'After all, it's about the only thing that has not gone up in price. Perhaps then we could walk in Tunbridge Wells without having to keep our eyes on the grounds.'

Am I to assume from the dog lovers' failure to reply to my letter that they have no substantial answer to my complaints?

STUART HAYES

September 9th, 1953

DOG PAEN

SIR – What a hard man your correspondent, Mr Stuart Hayes must be. How much he misses in life by not having a faithful doggie pal. I think children are a far worse nuisance that any dear little dog. Mr Hayes says that the dog tax should be trebled. That would be very unfair indeed as I think keeping a dog is quite expensive enough nowadays. Even if the fee did go up, I would not lose my little pal. I would sooner starve myself than see him go short.

DOG LOVER

September 10th, 1953

TAILING COPS

SIR – I am not sure who is putting forward the more ridiculous case – Stuart Hayes, who wants to treble dog licence fees, or 'Dog Lover' (how wise to remain anonymous), whose eulogy of doggie pals suggests that the writer is a psychopathic case. Dog Lover, who would rather starve than see his/her pet go short, and who reckons that children are more nuisance than dogs (Picasso causes more nuisance than atom-bombs!) really deserves no answer. But Mr Hayes is more logical. I would however, suggest that his 'remedy' for an undoubted nuisance is bound to be ineffectual. The very people who cause most trouble with their disgusting quadrupeds are just those who would willingly pay three times as much for the privilege.

Adequate enforcement of existing by-laws is all that is necessary.

LAW AND ORDER

September 16th, 1953

LOITERING DOGS

SIR – Is it not time that something was done about dogs running loose in the streets? I raise this point as a motorist who has thrice in the last two days had reason to curse these uncontrolled animals. I am sure no member of the motoring community would willingly kill or harm a dog. In fact, I feel that instinct would be against this. But should the animal be killed or maimed a report is required of the whole incident. Surely, in return, the police or some like body should be empowered to round up all unleashed dogs and action taken against their owners.

MOTORIST

January 27th, 1954

45

Animals at Large

All animals find generous support in Tunbridge Wells
– except, perhaps, the ones that are heard as well as
seen. Towns people assiduously patrol the thin blue line
that runs through creatures large and small.

LOUD COCKS

SIR – Now that lighter mornings are before us, may I remind your readers who keep poultry that cock-crowing at dawn in the neighbourhood of houses, especially in a town, constitutes a nuisance, and a very real annoyance to many people... The owner of a dog that barks all night is liable to be summoned, but the owner of a cock which crows unceasingly from 2.30 a.m. overlooks the fact that he is keeping a far greater nuisance...

LIGHT SLEEPER

April 16th, 1915

VILE PLUMAGE

SIR – May I beg the favour of a space in your columns to protest against the revival of the cruel fashion of trimming women's hats with the plumage of ospreys and other beautiful birds, and at the same time make an appeal to all women and girls not to wear them. It is now some years since the practice was whole-heartedly condemned, through the columns of the Press, by all humane people, so the present younger generation of girls may not know that it means the horrible torturing of these exquisite and perfectly helpless little creatures whose feathers are torn from their bodies while they are still alive. But the details are too sickening to dwell upon.

I will merely point out that it is a crime of the meanest and most contemptible kind, and one against which every right-minded person should protest. It is also an insult to the better feelings and

47

intelligence of the girls of the present day to think that for the sake of their personal adornment they will consent to participate in anything so low down and repulsive. It is a quite unnecessary fashion that is sprung upon us from time to time. We don't ask for it, and we don't want it, so let us consistently and persistently refuse to accept it whenever it re-appears. It is a merely money-making scheme, and if we do this, those who are responsible for it will be forced to turn their brains into other and less revolting directions in search of new fashions. Nothing can be said in its defence.

AMY WOODBURN

May 2nd, 1919

CALLOW SLAUGHTER

SIR – I do so heartily agree with the letter signed 'Nancy Baldwin' in this week's *Advertiser* re pictures of calves to be sold for slaughter at the Tonbridge market. I did not see them till later in the week but it roused in me also a feeling of nausea and strong disgust. I cannot understand how such pictures can be found amusing or entertaining, and I fail to see why a little creature, two days old, should be called stubborn or made the subject of poking and laughter. Are we really the nation of animal lovers that we profess to be?

And what of the children? – Are they to be brought up to regard these scenes as 'funny,' with no pity or mercy for the helplessness of these baby creatures? I may be sentimental, but I would rather be sentimental than callow. Please may I ask you to discourage the insertion of such pictures in your otherwise worthy paper.

ETHEL GRACE WELLS

July 28th, 1954

[Editor's note: – It is not the function of this newspaper to suppress facts but to reveal them as they are.]

HUNTING TICKS

SIR – Now that the regular hunting season is beginning, may I, through the medium of your columns, request everyone who hunts with the West Kent Hounds to exercise particular care not to damage crops? Owing to the very wet state of the country, even wheat may be seriously injured by being ridden over, and fruit may be irreparable.

There is so much keep everywhere this year, that stock will be left in the fields later than usual, and it is therefore more than ever reprehensible to leave gates open.

Finally, I would ask ladies and gentlemen to restrain their ardour for jumping fences until hounds are running.

J.W.B. WHITE.

November 13th, 1903

A SPURIOUS MANGLE

SIR – Will you kindly grant me the use of your columns to call attention to a sport which will soon

49

recommence in some parts of the country? I refer to the hunting of park-deer. These animals are conveyed to the meet in a van. They are turned up in districts with which they are unacquainted. They are chased several times each season. Being practically domesticated, they do not know how to protect themselves from the pursuing pack. Though the hunters do not wish to kill them, their quarry runs with the fear of death pervading it. They seek refuge, when it is possible, in yards and sheds, and in a cottage scullery. If the hunt staff are not up when the stag gives in, a mangling scene is enacted.

We think this sport is cruel and demoralising. What is the use, we would ask, of spending vast sums upon education, when such an example of inhumanity is set to the young by adults?

We would venture to suggest that persons who witness this kind of hunting should expose it in the Press, and thus assist Mr Corrie Grant to get the Spurious Sport Bill enacted, which would not only suppress tame-deer chasing, but also rabbit coursing and shooting birds from traps.

J. STRATTON

October 7th, 1904

KARMIC KILLINGS

SIR – In these days of sports kill-joys, Red Flag processions and Communist serenading, not forgetting the depressing weather of late, may I ask you and your readers to join with me in welcoming 1926 by blotting out the memory of all the aforesaid unpleasant subjects and picture instead a lovely morning of sunshine (Monday, January 4th), a meet of our well-known pack, under the excellent mastership of Miss Styles, at the charming residence of Ashurst Park, when Major Field-Marsham and Mrs Field-Marsham, in true English fashion, gave a hearty welcome to all. To crown the glorious meeting, Reynard was soon found at home, and gave a rousing run.

OLD DOG FOX

January 8th, 1926

FOXING FOXES

SIR – I am not exactly a lover or a condoner of fox-hunting, but it occurs to me that the people who wrote to you last week protesting against the 'kill' in a Rusthall street are taking rather an unreasonable attitude.

As I read the facts, the 'kill' was made some time before the Hunt arrived on the scene, and therefore there can be no suggestion that the spectacle was deliberately staged or that the fox was hunted into the street for the express purpose of being killed there. Obviously the whole thing was entirely accidental, from the point of view of the hunt, yet your correspondents seem to consider it was done for the purpose.

I would not mind wagering that not one of your correspondents saw what happened, and that they are merely protesting against something about which they have been told. From enquiries I have made,

51

none of the residents in the vicinity have any objections to what happened – in fact, very few of them saw the occurrence, and certainly it was not witnessed by children. Even if it were, it is no worse than children witnessing a rather bad road accident – a far more frequent occurrence and, in my experience, something greatly enjoyed by them.

One wonders what the feelings of your correspondents towards the 'poor, innocent, defenceless fox' would be if they kept chickens and had their stocks depleted by a series of nightly raids. Quite murderous, no doubt, bearing in mind what usually happens when the neighbour's dog starts trampling down the flower beds!

FAIR PLAY

February 24th, 1939

HALF-COCK HUNT

SIR – What a pity the Eridge Hunt 'muffled' its great opportunity of showing the town the full pageantry of Britain's greatest field sport. An enormous crowd turned up at the fair ground on Boxing Day full of enthusiasm for the hunt and hoping to see everything that went on.

What did most of them actually see? Just a great throng of bystanders, with the odd horse and rider peeping above the struggling mass of people. On the move off, I doubt if one person in fifty saw anything at all. No one knew which way the hunt would go. Many hundreds lined Major York's Hull in a hope of catching sight of the hounds, huntsman and riders as they moved off. They were disappointed.

Why was the direction in which the hunt would go kept such a dark secret? It was a great anti-climax when the field disappeared through the woods and down to the Eridge Road, taking the majority of spectators entirely by surprise. Let us have another meet next Boxing Day on the fair ground – but let the hunt move off up Major York's Road so the thousands of spectators can really see something.

FOOT-FOLLOWER
December 30th, 1953

HUNTING BAN

SIR – Hare hunting has resumed in your district.

Over 400 year ago Sir Thomas More denounced this sport as 'the meanest, vilest, most abject form of butchery.'

Two hundred years later William Blake wrote: 'Each outcry of hunted hare, a fibre from the brain doth tear,' and William Somerville described the end when, 'with infant screams, she yields her breath and there reluctant dies.'

There are still those who are so insensitive to suffering that they can find their 'amusement' in such sport.

We often wonder if they would be so enthusiastic about it were the roles of hunter and hunted reversed.

J. C. SHARP
November 18th, 1953

53

Disorderly Disasters

*Visiting the pleasant and green jewel that is Tunbridge Wells
you might think it is paradise. Not so, it is at the mercy of
tsunami of alcohol. Everywhere its nefarious effects can be
felt, aided and abetted by false kindness.*

AWFUL EVIL GROCERS

SIR – For years I have felt it my duty to attend at Court when the annual Brewster Sessions are held, and licenses are applied for, as it is thought that the presence of ladies on such unpleasant occasions has the effect of influencing Magistrates not to grant fresh licenses. But there is still one matter, in some respects as important, if not more so.

I refer to the grocers' licence. This is the cause of untold mischief among women, it is so easy for the shopkeeper to enter on his bill a few more pounds of tea, sugar, &c., and not enter the bottles of spirits and wine at all, so that should the good man of the house be sufficiently domesticated to look at the grocers' bills, there is nothing to which he can possibly object. A case of this sort came under my own observation, the poor deluded husband not finding out till too late, that she who ought to have been his help-mate, thus brought disgrace to his once happy home, a perfect scandal to the children and servants.

This awful evil exists among a certain class, who would not think of going to the public-house. No effort is being made to secure the refusal of this most objectionable license. Is it not time something was done in this matter, which has caused more harm than will ever be known? Why not get up petitions in our different constituencies, and send them to our respective representatives in Parliament, begging them to have the Grocers' License Act rescinded?

A.B.

February 6th, 1903

BOARD UP HELL

SIR – I notice the Camden Hotel, which, with its adjoining premises, covers a large space next to the Town Hall, is to be offered for sale. From the fact that it occupies a unique spot, in a populous part of the town, and where there is a great deal of traffic, I suppose there will be a keen competition to acquire it, because it is naturally a rendezvous for drinking, although, from what I hear, I believe the place is respectably conducted. Still, this does not alter the fact that a great deal of drinking, which is admittedly the curse of the country, goes on which would be stopped if the place as a public-house were closed up.

Consequently, I should much like to see the premises bought by one or more practical Christians, in order to close it for once and ever as a place which leads to mental and physical deterioration, and I, who have studied the drink question for many years, and seen the manifold evils which follow in its train, earnestly hope that a noble and successful effort will be made to acquire the property and convert it to some better use municipal or otherwise.

AN ABSTAINER

August 24th, 1906

RUFFIAN OUTRAGE

SIR – Is it not time that the authorities of Tunbridge Wells did something to lessen the disgraceful scenes so frequently to be witnessed after dark on the Pantiles, which seems to be the nightly meeting place of the undesirable of both sexes, not only of the town, but its immediate neighbourhood? As an instance of how little attention is paid to this scandal by those who ought to make the respectability of the town their chief aim, it seems that for some time on Saturday night only one policeman was present to cope with three or four drunken ruffians, with the result that he had a bad time until assistance arrived. There is no town in the South of England where such disgraceful conduct is to be seen as that on the Pantiles on Sunday nights, it being quite impossible for any lady to use that thoroughfare, and I have heard visitors express their astonishment at what they have seen and likewise that a town such as Tunbridge Wells could allow such disreputable gatherings to take place. No doubt, Mr Editor, you will use the influence of your paper to draw the attention of those in authority to this long neglected scandal.

RATEPAYER

June 7th, 1907

LEMONADE PLONKERS

SIR – We hear it said sometimes that it is unfair to rob the poor man of his beer when the rich man can indulge in intoxicating drinks at his pleasure.

According to the Bishop of London, the rich man has learned the value of total abstinence, and more, 'it is quite fashionable to be a teetotaller.' The bishop said the other day that when he attended a public function he found a number of teetotallers. In the city the waiters were quite used to plonking down his tankard of lemonade, and there would be Lord Roberts on one side and Lord Methuen on the other sharing the Bishop's lemonade. 'Public opinion was coming round to their side, and not the least of their victories was the conversion of the doctors.'

Mr Haldane, when speaking recently at the annual meeting of the Royal Army Temperance Association, said: – 'Our young officers more and more called for lemonade instead of whiskey and champagne. That meant that soldiers were beginning to realise the enormous waste of intellectual, moral, and physical force that drink produced in the past.'

Sir Victor Horsley has pointed out that total abstinence, so far from being a stupid fad, is the course which both science and common-sense dictate. Surely in face of the above testimonies we may hope that the day is fast approaching when the majority of our people will accept Sir Victor Horsley's verdict.

GOOD HEALTH

July 5th, 1907

WILD BIRDS

SIR – A correspondent signing herself 'Observer' writes in the *Daily Chronicle* as follows: – 'As a Colonial, I should like to ventilate my views on this degrading habit of women drinking in public-houses. Can these poor, miserable specimens of humanity, whom one sees inside and hanging around outside the public-house of the poorer districts of London really be my own country-women? Are they not the dregs of some inferior, yet unknown savage race? Would that some noble-minded legislator would take up the cause! Therein lies the only remedy. Prohibit women from using public-houses. It is no use appealing to the better nature (that is drowned in drink, so to speak) of this class of women. In the Colony I am acquainted with women who are never seen in the public-house.'

Alas! nothing can save this nation if its women continue their present drinking habits. When will mothers realise that they are doing a baby a cruel wrong if they themselves take alcoholic liquor even in moderation, before the birth of the child or while nursing it?

One question more. When will brewers and publicans show a patriotic spirit and say, 'we will discourage drinking among women by refusing to serve them with drink, for we realise that drinking mothers can never rear a healthy, sober nation'? Are there no 'noble-minded' men in the Liquor Trade, or has the greed of gold killed every humane and patriotic instinct in their hearts? Why should the welfare of this country, nay, its very existence, be sacrificed. England protects her wild birds and hares; why not her helpless babies?

A BRITISH WOMAN

October 1st, 1909

WICKED PRIZES

SIR – I much regret to see again in the list of prizes to the Territorials published in the *Advertiser* of yesterday's issue, casks of ale, whiskey, port wine, and sherry. Surely every soldier knows that alcohol does not help a man shoot straight, or march well? 'The whole crowd of the Roosevelt,' said the mate, 'from Commander Perry, Captain Bob, and downward, all worked and laid stress on Temperance principles. They could face 60 below zero and all their hardships better without alcohol.'

If alcohol is not required amid the hardships of North Pole, surely our Territorials do not require it....

E.E.H.

December 30th, 1911

INTEMPERATE LETTERS

SIR – Apparently teetotalism, whatever else it may do, does not make for good temper, judging from the last letter of the Secretary of the 33-year-old Kent Temperance Federation, about which I was 'impertinent' enough to make a few caustic observations. Really, Mr Whyte, if your letters are representative of the views of your society, I imagine it has outlived its usefulness, and I don't think the county of Kent would suffer one iota if it were disbanded to-morrow.

In fact, it might gain, for, as I pointed out previously, if the thousands of pounds it gets through during the course of a few years were spent on furniture, boots, clothing or even beer, it would provide more employment than if spent on teetotal propaganda. As this, Mr Whyte, is your own line of argument, you won't, I am sure, object to my applying it personally to you.

W.P. HAMMOND

March 31st, 1923

BLUE-STOCKING ARMAGEDDON

SIR – A great war is in the first stage of growth. One hundred millions of the United States of America are being rapidly divided into two hostile camps. Who are working to divide them? Men who desire to compel a whole nation to live without the privilege which has always hitherto been a birthright – the privilege of having a 'comforting drink' when age or worry or sadden sickness needs it.

The whole history of the world illustrates this fact, that fanatics, who are governed more by imagination than judgement, will fight to the death! The threat is arising that soldiers will be employed to coerce if the civil authorities fail to succeed in enforcing prohibition.

In the coming meeting on the Common we do not want to hear how the League of Nations has saved America from bankruptcy by lending her British money, nor that Poles and Germans are doing in Silesia. These are small matters. The great question of the day is, what can the League of Nations do to arrest the horrors of a great civil war in the United States, a war which will profoundly affect the whole world, and especially ourselves.

CALEB EDWARDS

23, Culverden Park Road

July 6th, 1923

FREE B&BS

SIR – The Chief Constable's report on convictions for drunkenness in Tunbridge Wells for 1937 should bring about careful inquiries. Thirty-three persons were proceeded against for drunkenness – thirteen more than in 1936, which was an increase on the previous year. Compared with other towns, Tunbridge Wells shows up badly. Tonbridge with a population of just under half ours, had only five convictions; Canterbury, 10; Maidstone, 17; Ramsgate, 12.

One notices that 17 were vagrants, not residents. They come to our town, create a disturbance, resist the police, and get one day! No wonder we have an increase. I am told the men pass on this leniency to their friends, with the result that they patronize us with their unwelcome presence.

When 'run-in' for being drunk and disorderly, they receive a good supper, bed and breakfast, and go on their way rejoicing. No wonder they come!

Twenty years ago, owning to increase of drunkenness here, the Bench decided to send these men to prison, and the trouble abated. Surely this should be done now.

RATEPAYER

February 18th, 1938

The Next Generation

The jeunesse dorée of Tunbridge Wells will no doubt blossom into the town's glorious future. Meanwhile, there is some debate as to their nature and how best to educate them. Caning – anyone?

SCHOOL REIGN OF TERROR

SIR – My excuse for troubling you with the fact that the proper training of our children is not only a local, but a national concern. In the part of the country from which I write a virtual reign of terror existed, accompanied by a not very edifying conflict between parents and teachers. One of the successful candidates at a recent School Board election went so far as to state in his circular that complaints not alone of physical, but also of verbal ill-usage, were frequent, and I believe a leading medical practitioner in the same district has been much exercised in endeavouring to find, or invent, a suitable word to describe a new form of illness among children attending a certain school, which is somewhat of the nature of jaundice, and which is supposed to be induced by fright and injudicious punishments. Surely this is a lamentable state of affairs in a civilized and Christian country.

PATER FAMILIAS

June 19th, 1903

CANING

SIR – I have had an education of twenty years, and have been also a manager of large schools. I thank those gentlemen who have written ably against the above. I know the ill effect of the present rules as to corporal punishment in London Board Schools. Is it not most pitiable to see mere babies, six years of age and under, caned by women because they happened (many of them under-fed) to whisper to each other

64

during a dull lesson or were a little late, or came with a soiled hand? What other methods of discipline are ever reverted to but the cane? The cane seems to be the ever ready resort of teachers of children, whose large and burly hands should surely have better employment than inflicting a cruel punishment in addition to the many hardships characteristic of the child life of our cities and towns.

> **B.A., LL.D.**
>
> July 10th, 1903

A FEW STROKES WON'T HURT

SIR – The 'Mater' who wrote last week about corporal punishment will probably find that her information is exaggerated. As for the thrashed Americanite, who said he was not crying because his whacking hurt, but because of the insult to American citizens, if he had been my son he should have had a little more, to remove falsehood from his lips of insufferable priggishness from his brain. However, he need not argue about a myth.

Perhaps 'Mater' does not know what corporal punishment means. It is punishment of the body, and a couple of strokes wisely administered do less harm to the body than detention in polluted air, solitary, sulky, confinement, or letting a boy neglect his physical exercises.

I never went home when I was a boy and told my mother, my dear sensible mother, that I had been whacked at school. I was afraid of several things – a little afraid of hurting her feelings, very much of

65

getting a second dose, also of hearing my father say he was glad to hear it, it would do me good, besides the danger of my schoolmaster (wonderful mixture of firmness and kindness) taking his turn at telling tales out of school.

PATER

August 11th, 1905

FADDISM

SIR – Referring to your leaderette of last week on Miss Fowler-Tutt's paper on 'Our Education system,' I must be allowed to take exception to one expression of years, viz. 'The teachers of this country need to be taught how to teach.' This, I hold, sir, is a libel on the character and capabilities of a hardworking and capable set of men and women. The teachers can teach. The fault lies in the originators of our systems and schemes of education, who do not know how to originate a scheme, for they allow the schools to be exploited by the faddist, and while they give full scope to the fad, they lose sight of the ultimate aim.

CHAS. M. MALPASS

President of the Tonbridge District N.U.T. Association

34, North Farm Road,

May 27th, 1910

MODERN TEACHERS

SIR – I was shocked to read in 'The Diary of a Man

66

About 'Town' last week that two schoolmistresses had been found ripping 'palm' from bushes on the Common.

This is rather indicative to me of an irresponsible trend among some young teachers today. No wonder many children are so badly behaved.

So much stress is laid upon education but I cannot help feeling that modern teachers are not of the same calibre as those when I was a child.

Like the children, they seem to take advantage of the lack of discipline and set poor examples to the younger generation. Perhaps all this psychology nonsense is the cause.

FATHER

September 5th, 1912

SCOTCH ADVICE

SIR – Young men who wish to get on in the world should read Andrew Carnegie's book *The Empires of Business*. In it he gives young men much good advice. He is as everyone knows, a Scotchman, son of weaver, and his father was too poor to do more for him than give him a sound constitution, tremendous energy, and industry, 'iron principles of right and wrong and the fear of God.' At the age of fourteen Andrew went to America and got a post as a stoker in some engineering works in America, and has made his £400,000,000. The advice of such a man is worth heeding.

I note the following. Speaking of alcohol he says: – 'Resolve never to touch it, except at meals; but I implore you hold it inconsistent with the dignity and self-respected of gentlemen, with what is due from yourselves to yourselves, to drink a glass of liquor at a bar. Be far too much of a gentleman ever to enter a bar-room ... I beseech you avoid liquor, speculation, and endorsement. Do not fail in either, for liquor and speculation are the Scylla and Charybdis of the young man's business sea.'

A READER

September 11th, 1903

HAVE WE LOST OUR MIND?

SIR – A paragraph appeared last week in the 'Daily Mail' headed 'Civilisers wanted.' The writer describes all too vividly the awful conditions of his parish, one part of which – 'a veritable plague spot' – contains 30 public houses, *i.e.*, one to every 150 of the population, including children. Mr Justice Grantham, when charging the Grand Jury at Surrey Assizes last week, said the calendar disclosed an amount of depravity among young children which was 'most melancholy.'

'No money about' is the despairing cry this summer in almost every trade and profession. Everyone is feeling the pinch – except the drink traffic. The country manages to find £170,000,000 odd a year to spend on drink. In the first nine months of last year 60,861 recruits were medically inspected, and only 29,500 were finally approved. Many of those rejected were 'deficient in height and chest measurement, and lacked stamina.'

Our youths are growing up sickly stunted men; and clergy, judges, and doctors tell us it is chiefly due to the drink traffic and yet — — ? We are to do nothing to rectify this gigantic evil, unless we can compensate the public handsomely. But a man who starts, say, chemical or any other works, which prove to be injurious to the health of the neighbourhood, gets notice to quit, and no compensation is given him.

Are we really sane? Has the greed for gold killed all humane, reasonable sentiments in the minds of men who boast that they are British born?

SADLY PUZZLED

August 5th, 1904

RULES, ANYONE?

SIR – Can anything be done to preserve the beautiful Grove, and keep it (as it ought to be), a pleasant resort for inhabitants and visitors?

The boys and girls walk anywhere but on the paths, they climb the young trees, and break off the branches. A boy was seen to climb one of the new lamp-posts and deliberately pull the by-pass up and down for sheer mischief.

The excellent paths are widened in some parts several feet, quite spoiling the look of the Grove. The bandstand is over-run with children. Lately the seats have been painted, but already they have been trodden on, and will soon be in the disgraceful state they were last summer.

There are many good rules and regulations in very small type, neatly framed and high up, but they have no effect on lawless children, who wilfully destroy and mis-use the place meant for their pleasure and recreation, as well as for others.

A RESIDENT

March 31st, 1905

LECTURE IMPURE LONDON YOUTH

SIR – We are making an earnest appeal on behalf of the work which is being undertaken amongst the young men of London, especially among those who live in the large business houses of the City…It is very difficult to exaggerate the dangers and temptations which make it hard for these young fellows to keep pure in the midst of London life. The corruption of young men and boys has assumed quite terrible proportions, and the work of rescue is no longer confined to women and girls.

The Committee are quite convinced that a great effort must be made to save and protect them, and to raise a higher standard of purity amongst them. If we are to have a cleaner England, we must begin with the young men. It is obvious that no detailed and sensational accounts can be given of the work, but during the past five years more than 700 lectures and addresses have been delivered, and hundreds of young men have been helped back to purity of life (largely by hep and sympathy of Mr Percy Taylor, the Agent of the City Committee…)

A.J. Ind, President

F.E. Kerwsick, Chairmen of Committee

December 16th, 1910

LOUTISH LOOTERS

SIR – Re your remarks on 'Juvenile depravity,' I can supplement them from my own experience of a small tradesman, who told me how he was being victimised by an organised gang of juveniles, who visit small shops, and spend perhaps 2d., and pilfer 1s. or more. The modus operandi is for two of them to give an order for something in the shop, and during the serving, when the attention of the shopkeeper is engaged, the others take anything handy…

FIAT JUSTITIA
March 8th, 1912

TINY HOOLIGANS

SIR – On behalf of many residents of High Brooms, I would like to draw your attention to the disgraceful hooliganism on the part of gangs of small youths.

It is rapidly becoming almost impossible to hold meetings or do anything of a public nature without interference. There seems also a mania for throwing oddments at any window which dares to show a light after dark.

This only seems to have commenced since the authorities at Tonbridge saw fit to replace the police here by freshmen. Perhaps if these new men were provided with guide books they might occasionally find their way around the

71

Southborough portion of High Brooms after dark.

EVA BRICK

March 27th, 1925

HEFTY GIRLS

SIR – I am astonished to see your report of the West Kent Stoolball League that the girls of Rusthall and Tunbridge Wells find it impossible to play on their respective Commons owing to the hooliganism and rude behaviour of boys and youths who frequent such places. What a reproach to Royal Tunbridge Wells!!

Have we no police or common-keepers?

Perhaps if these hefty girls took the law into their own hands once or twice, and protected themselves, it would be better.

DISGUSTED

April 15th, 1927

INTOLERABLE PAMPERING

SIR – The pampering of the young which is going on today, paying everything for them, and dressing them up in uniforms as the youth movements do is fatal to the future of this country. Let them fight their own battles, as generations past have done. Many of young are sadly lacking now in manners and self-control – soon they will become intolerable.

M.E. WELLDON

March 30th, 1945

SHORT SHRIFT

SIR – As a southerner, I would normally have been among the first to fight against S. Raymond's allegation of 'southern rudeness,' but now I have had an object lesson.

In a midlands town last week, I passed three juvenile train-spotters on a railway footbridge. I was a stranger to them, but each smiled and said, 'Good afternoon, sir.'

In Tunbridge Wells a few days earlier, I had to pass through a gate on which three lads of about the same age were sitting. They did not get off, but regaled me with the greeting, 'Wotcher, shorty.' As I walked off, I was hit in the back by a stone.

DISILLUSIONED
September 16th, 1953

BUS BOY-ETIQUETTE

SIR – In connection with the recent correspondence suggesting that certain bus conductors are not showing consideration towards potential schoolboy travellers, I thought that possibly you might be interested in the following extracts from the rule book of Devonport and District Tramways, published in the eighteen-fifties. This rule book called for 'Honesty! Punctuality! Obedience! Sobriety! Civility! And Alertness!'

Motormen and conductors should be 'attentive to duty, carefully observing every person as they proceed along the streets, and if they notice anyone standing looking at cars, undecided whether or not to ride, make a motion with their hands to attract their attention, which would in many cases attract them to ride.'

Conductors were to give passengers 'kindly explanations' and adopt any course rather than keep passengers waiting for change. Inspectors carried change 'for at least a shilling.' If two tramcars met on a single line, the drivers of both were to be to blame unless one could prove the other wrong.

KENNETH WARREN

January 20th, 1954

BOY-BEDLAM BUSES

SIR – Every day it is my misfortune to travel on the 12.08 p.m. bus from Central Station to Rusthall – and it is gradually becoming a nightmare ride. The majority of my travelling companions are a rugged bunch of screaming, shouting, ill-mannered, abusive schoolboys.

Every day, except at week-ends, it is my fate to ride home to Rusthall on 12.08 and every day I meet up with these little Giles-like characters who make the journey a complete nightmare.

They clamber over the seats; fight on the floor; whistle; stamp over the upholstery; shout; throw paper bags – and generally annoy everybody riding with them. The unfortunate thing is that nobody seems to dare say a word against these little hooligans.

74

I have been using this particular bus for over two months, and only twice during that time have I seen a conductor use his authority in getting the children to be quiet.

Let me give you the diary of events on a 'normal' 12.08 p.m. run from Tunbridge Wells to Rusthall.

12.05. – I arrive at 81 bus stop opposite Central Station; everything quiet.

12.08. – Bus to Rusthall arrives. I get aboard. Downstairs it is full, so I start to climb to the top deck. Three little boys are trying to throttle a fourth by pushing his head back over the seat. Two little girls look on admiringly.

12.10. – Bus reaches stop at King Charles Church. Outside big boys, little boys, thin boys, fat boys, ginger-haired boys, boys in school uniform, all sorts of little boys are trying to push the bus over. (Actually, they are trying to get aboard – but that is the impression.)

12.11. – The bus is a bedlam. The boys are joined by one or two little girls. The boys try to impress. Result? Chaos!

12.14. – Bus approaches Spa Hotel. I hear a 'pinging' noise. Something hits the glass pane beside my left ear. A piece of wet chewing gum drops on my coat.

12.15. – Two other boys push another off his seat. He bangs against the legs of a woman passenger.

12.16. – Bretland Road, Rusthall. A great cheer goes up. Workmen recently put up a glass screen

75

at the bus stop there. One pane is now missing. Whole upper deck congratulates unknown saboteur.

12.17. – Ride over. Remainder of mob stream off bus. One kicks at a stone. He makes contact – and the stone almost flies through a drapery store window. I creep gladly away to my lunch – and shudder at the thought of tomorrow's ride.

Where does the fault lie? With the bus company; the headmaster and teachers at the local schools, or the parents?

Personally I should be glad if the police or some other authority would lay on a vehicle with a specially padded interior to collect these little horrors from school. Then, at least, I would be able to travel home in comfort.

> A.J.C
>
> July 7th, 1954

HORRID HENRIES

SIR – As a very frequent visitor to your attractive town and an interested reader of the 'Advertiser,' may I make one or two observations on some aspects of local life which have lately struck me?

First, would it be possible for teachers, particularly of older boys, to give them some instruction on courtesy and manners affecting their conduct after leaving afternoon school?

Allowing for the natural exuberance of teenage lads, I think it is deplorable that some of them should be guilty of horse-play on tops of buses (carefully quietening down when the conductor makes his appearance) and of pushing about in bus queues – even barging ahead of their rightful turn when there is only an old lady in front. I have too often seen this done, also of flinging and catapulting of paper missiles at each other on bus tops.

As for the surreptitious smoking of cigarettes by boys obviously under the age of fourteen – well others may have noticed quite a bit of this going on and a policeman's wary eye might lead to the discomfiture of one or more of the offenders.

REGULAR VISITOR

October 27th, 1954

LONG ARM OF THE WICKED

SIR – The local electricity authorities must be getting tired of replacing the bulb in lamp No. 972 at the bottom of Culverden Down.

It is wilfully smashed, on the average, once a fortnight.

The other evening we passed some boys armed with long sticks just near the lamp and when we came back later the bulb was smashed again.

X.Y.Z.

July 14th, 1954

77

Ghastly Buses

Unlike any other place in pleasant Tunbridge Wells, people in buses are squashed together in a small confined airless space and at the mercy of their driver and fellow travellers. Is it surprising that feathers fly?

WILD BUSES

SIR – I have been requested to call attention, in the public interest, through the medium of your paper to the scandalous way in which the public are treated in connection with the Omnibus Service to Langton and Fordcombe. On Friday, December 29th, at least six persons (there may well have been more) were awaiting to go from Tunbridge Wells, by the Omnibus timed to start at six p.m. As no 'bus appeared, enquiry was made at the offices at the Great Hall.

Someone – a representative of the Company – rather jauntily informed all enquirers that there would be no omnibus, as there had been an accident, but 'there were plenty of cabs about'. The only pity is that they did not order one at the Company's expense.

As a result of this, I know for a fact that two women, perfect strangers to each other, one physically unable, the other too terrified to take so long a walk in the wet, cold, and dark night, after becoming thoroughly drenched in the rain, had to seek shelter at the house of one of them, in Tunbridge Wells, and there being no sleeping accommodation had to pass the night sitting by the fire.

On another wild night, the driver not having any passengers for Fordcombe, drove a little way through Langton, pulled up at a convenient and warm corner, and then turned leisurely back. How nice for passengers who might be waiting at Fordcombe!

I am relating facts, however, and will leave others to comment; but I would like to ask the Company's

79

representative one question. Would it not have paid the Company better in the end, if he had hired one of the many cabs he spoke of, rather than to insult those whom he knew could not afford it, by suggesting that they do so?

PRO BONO PUBLICO

January 12th, 1900

FOOTBALL MESS

SIR – Permit me to call attention to the so-called cheap excursion to London on Saturday last, advertised in connection with the final tie of the Football Cup. As you are aware, the kick-off was at 3.30, but to obtain a 3s. excursion ticket to London Bridge for the Palace one had to leave Tunbridge Wells at 8.17 a.m., while from Sevenoaks one could leave up to 11.14. Then on the return journey, which many would like to have made about 6 o'clock, the rule was that one could only travel by the 8.10 p.m.

The excursion was too dear, started too early, returned too late, gave no choice of trains, and was of little service. Cannot something better than this be done by the S.E. & C.R.? The L.B. & S.C.R. fixed more reasonable times for departure, but fixed the return journey also at 8.10 p.m.

If on Saturday the excursion was 3s. why should the usual Wednesday excursion be more?

TRAVELLER

April 17th, 1906

BAFFLING BUSES

SIR – I have recently come to this well-known resort with my family for the winter and having often a desire to avail myself of some of the Autocar services starting from the South Eastern Railway Station, I have been perplexed to know to what places these vehicles are bound.

Sometimes there are three of them together at the Station without the slightest indication on the cars where they are going to or time at which they start. Of course, the reply will be, 'Why don't you ask?' To this I answer, 'Why should it be necessary to do so?' I have as a matter of fact, done so, and have not always received a particularly polite answer. A stranger does not desire to learn from the cars only that the 'Opera House opens twice nightly.'

I have never been in any place yet where such cars are not distinctly labelled by a board or some such indicator as to their ultimate destination. One might as well have a lot of buses passing in the Mansion House, for instance, having nothing on them except perhaps 'Johnnie Walker's Whisky.'

A VISITOR
October 24th, 1919

PETROL PIRATES

SIR – May I draw attention to a matter which concerns the general public in this town and district,

The local Autocar Company have advanced their fare to one halfpenny a stage, owing, I gather, to the increase in the cost of petrol of 7d. a gallon.

81

I would be interested to know how many times over this halfpenny per passenger pays for the extra cost of petrol...

JUSTICE

September 22nd, 1920

IS PUNCTUALITY TOO MUCH TO ASK FOR?

SIR – Can anyone beat the Southern Railway S.E. and C.R. Section for slackness? I am one of the army of those who get to and from their work by rail. Twice during the last week the 9.45 a.m. from Wadhurst (down) – to mention only one train – has been an hour late, while the number of times it has been anything up to half an hour behind is considerable. On eventually arriving, it usually has three carriages, and very often one of them is reserved.

When it is remembered that there are no down trains from the station between 7.35 and 9.54 (over two hours), I really do think it is time the Railway Company began to consider the passengers by, at any rate, trying to keep to the time-tables. A letter to the Company complaining of these miserable conditions was answered in the usual way, viz., 'That the matter shall receive attention.' The attention that has been given is reflected in the fact that this morning (Wednesday), the train was 1 ¼ hours late. But, after all, it was only what one could expect.

There does not seem to be the least suggestion of business in this management, and I think the dilatory and altogether abominable way which the trains are run is such as to justify the utmost criticism.

F.C. BOORMAN

August 1st, 1924

COVER ERECTIONS

SIR – May I avail myself of the Britisher's privilege and register a grouse? After waiting many moons, the bus travelling public have at last been provided with queuing shelters near the War Memorial, but the granting of that belated concession has produced another cause for complaint. Half the pavement has now been taken up with the sort of Heath Robinson erections that support the shelters in one of Mount Pleasant's most congested spots.

Couldn't those responsible have gone the whole hog, and by making an appropriate indentation in the wall surrounding the Civic Centre, have kept the shelters clear of the pavement? Such a device would also have had the advantage of providing an opening to the main entrance to the Town Hall, thus obviating busy people having to negotiate the maze-like path that at present provides the other method of approach when one wants, for instance, to seek a little latitude re the electric light bill.

CONFIRMED GROUSER

April 16th, 1943

SICKENING WOMEN

SIR – On behalf of the men folk who, either having their hour's break for lunch, or, in many cases, having had sandwiches for the midday meal, wait for a bus to take them home to a well-earned hot meal, I protest that it is sickening to see the buses come in loaded chiefly with women returning from shopping during the lunch hour or between 5 p.m. and 6 p.m.

I, myself, this week on one occasion had to let five buses go and not until the sixth was I able to get on.

Another sore point is that whilst these men are still left to stand at King Charles stop, when the bus arrives at the Swan Hotel, four or five people get off and many a time the bus proceeds with empty seats. I suggest that the conductors, when they see a lot waiting, should be allowed to ask if there is anybody for the Swan, and, if so, request them to alight.

Then there are people who want Hungershall Park. To my idea this stop ought to be cut out in view of the fact that a person who needs Lower Green either has to get off at Bretland Road and walk along, or go to the High Street, Rusthall, and walk back.

I cast no blame on the company or its efficient staff. In fact, I give them great credit for the way they perform their duties most obligingly and with good manners, but I do feel our women folk should do as the company asks and travel earlier.

No doubt if you publish this a good many women will want to pull my hair out, but I take that chance, knowing full well the menfolk will agree I am correct.

So come along, ladies, look after your husband. Shop early and help him get home in comfort and good time.

R.T. CORDEN
December 5th, 1947

SHAMEFUL SLOW-POKES

SIR – How long does it take to travel by bus from St. John's Church to the Central Station? Five minutes at the most, you'd say.

You'll be lucky – I say you'll be lucky!

Because if you're unlucky (as I was the other day) you'll find it takes twice that. Fortunately I wasn't trying to catch a train.

This is how it goes. At the top of Grosvenor Hill the bus stops. Driver and conductor get off and you sit and wait for the replacement crew to walk along from the depot.

When they eventually loom into sight they aren't hurrying. Why should they (they would probably say if asked); the bus isn't due to leave until 11:20, or whatever time the 93 is scheduled at that point. It arrived ahead of schedule.

Eventually the 93 starts off down Grosvenor Hill and pulls up at the Memorial. The new conductor gets off and walks back to transact some important business at the M. and D. office.

Another two minutes wait. Eventually, after covering a mile in ten minutes, the passenger reaches his destination.

Has the M. & D. Company a high-paid PR to explain why fare-paying passengers must be treated in this way?

In the circumstances, my signature must obviously be:

DISGUSTED

March 24th, 1954

85

Honestly ...

It is well-known that Tunbridge Wells is a bastion of common sense and rectitude. But some inhabitants, really… You can't expect anyone to behave without putting them firmly in their place first.

DRIVING MANIAC

SIR – Would you allow me space in your valuable paper to suggest to the powers that be the desirability of erecting a street refuge at Ye Five Ways, or failing this, to endeavour in some way to impress upon the minds of the drivers across this dangerous junction the urgent necessity of exercising a little more regard to pedestrians than is the practice at the present time?

My attention was forcibly drawn to this on Monday shortly before one o'clock. The road was full of traffic when a lady driving a high-stepping horse in a dog cart, dashed across from Calverley Road towards Mount Ephraim Road, and in her mad haste, nearly ran over a postal telegraph boy, who was crossing at right angles on a bicycle. The lad barely escaped, but in so doing collided with me, who was on foot, with the result that we both fell, fortunately beyond the shaking neither was much hurt, but the lady (?) with the characteristic insolence of her class, drove on, never pausing to enquire if anyone was hurt.

Of course, I am not prepared to maintain that it would have mattered much if a common workman and a telegraph boy had been killed. But unless some means are adopted to prevent this sort of thing going on possibly some really important person, an alderman or a member of the Ratepayers' League, might get killed , and that would be far too heavy a price to pay.

THOS. E. COX

October 13th, 1905

UPSIDE-DOWN FLAGS

SIR – It is really surprising to find, in this present year of grace, how few Englishmen or Britons there are who know there is a right and a wrong way to 'fly' our 'National Flag.' – the Union Jack. Apparently they forget there is a right and a wrong to everything. Last Friday – being Empire Day – I went, out of curiosity, through our principal thoroughfares to see how many Union Jacks I could find flying upside down.

Of course, as expected, I found heaps. Even the Constitutional Club, Calverley Road, and the Conversation Club, Camden Road, were among the number. Doubtless one would expect them to know better; to make matters worse they won't listen to reason. Anyone being in doubt which is the correct way, I advise them to examine the flag, when flying at the Town Hall, or the one at Messers Upson's, Calverley Road.

Possibly a few if they examined for ever, may not discover one iota of difference. I will explain. At the left hand corner a broad strip of white is correct. In nine cases out of ten you find the narrow strip of white on top, and the broad beneath, which is wrong.

W.J. CORBYN

May 31st, 1907

FACE THE MUSIC

SIR – As a lover of music I should like to enter a protest against the time of our season band being utilized for such things as these so-called 'musical competitions.' I for one fail to see what amusement is in it, also what the object is. Not twenty per cent of the audiences take any interest in them, as was shown by the number which entered, and in the opinion of good musicians, and bringing their performance down to the level of a third-rate music hall.

Enough time of the band is already wasted in the evenings by the concert party, and surely the Band Committee can raise sufficient funds for the season's entertainments without resort to cheap advertisement such as this.

I should suggest that if these gentlemen cannot think of some other scheme, more edifying, they should all resign before next season and give place to others with higher ideals.

ONE DISGUSTED

September 20th, 1907

ROUTE ALL COMMUNISTS

SIR – Being present at the unveiling of the plaque on Thursday last week on the Pantiles I was surprised when the National Anthem was played to see that in a place like Tunbridge Wells which is noted for its loyalty and calls itself 'Royal' there should be people who refused to remove their hats.

Are such people Communists? If they are, Tunbridge Wells should be no place for such as they. We can do without them.

'IMPERIALIST'

June 14th, 1929

DEPRAVED PRACTICES

SIR – the Health Committee of Tunbridge Wells desire to appeal to all citizens to help stop the writing of objectionable matter on the walls of public conveniences.

They realised that these things are the work of depraved and deficient minds, and therefore they ask with the greater confidence for the co-operation of all decent-minded people.

If any person who witnesses the offence such as I have described will give information to the police, appropriate action will be taken against the offender.

R.M. BAKER

Chairman

February 20th, 1931

CYCLE TERRORISTS

SIR – Why are boys and others allowed to dash up and down the streets and around the corners of Tunbridge Wells without ringing their bells or giving other audible warning of their approach? In the early evening the danger is increased owing to the fact that no lamps are carried, and, if carried, not lighted. On many occasions lately I have nearly been knocked down by people riding cycles, and yet I am not blind, or deaf! But one is often unaware of their approach until something flashes past you within a few inches. A slip, a moment of hesitation – and the ambulance would be in request.

Have we no police, or are they too busy looking after the motors to notice such small fry as bicycles? One has only to read the local news each week to see the number of accidents caused by cyclists.

PENNY FARTHING

January 20th, 1933

LOUTISH MOTHERS

SIR – Having been a resident in Tonbridge only a few months, and coming from a much bigger town, I feel I must write to you about the selfish and unthinking women who congest the pavements of the High Street with their perambulators.

Frequently I, an elderly man, have had to step into the road to get past when two mothers have been either wheeling their infants side by side or have stopped to chat.

Surely these women realise the obstruction they are causing? If they cannot be more considerate perhaps the police could give them a sharp reminder sometimes. One of these days someone will be knocked down through stepping off the pavement into the road to get round a perambulator.

R. SAUNDERS

March 24th, 1954

THE REVOLTING ELDERLY

SIR – I am disgusted with the outbreak by R. Saunders ('Advertiser' last week) against mothers with prams who cause him inconvenience.

Perhaps this 'elderly man' would care to try a full day of housework, shopping, caring for children etc., and then see if he still thinks they are selfish. Trudging along with a pram and a load of shopping is no relaxation.

Mr Saunders should be glad to give way to pram-pushing mothers on the pavement.

His opinion is the thoughtless utterance of one who obviously cares for little but his own comfort.

> Yours etc.,
> **SELFISH WOMAN**
> March 31st, 1954

GOSSIPING MENACES

SIR – What an unparalleled piece of impertinence 'Selfish Woman's' letter was in last week's 'Advertiser.'

Just because a previous correspondent rightly pointed out that prams caused congestion – and danger – in shopping streets, he is labelled 'thoughtless' and 'selfish.'

'Selfish Woman' – what an apt pseudonym, by the way – says he should be glad to give way to pram-pushing mothers on the pavement.

But what about these thoughtless women who draw up two prams alongside one another and gossip endlessly, while other members of the public risk accidents by having to step in the gutter to pass?

I say they are a menace. They should be fined for obstructing the footway, just as a motorist who 'double parked' would be fined for holding up other vehicles.

Bah! Let them bulldoze their way down crowded pavements with their bloated baby carriages at their own risk when I'm around!

MISOGYNIST

April 7th, 1954

BOORISH MEN

SIR – The recent correspondence in the 'Advertiser' about pram-pushing mothers gives rise to another question.

Are the men of today completely lacking in chivalry and good manners? The 'elderly man' who first complained about the 'selfish women' would seem to suggest an answer in the affirmative. Have the days gone when a man, far from complaining about his own inconvenience, would politely step aside and allow a pram-pushing mother to pass?

There is a notable lack of this kind of courtesy today and I am sure that most women will agree that gentlemen are not what they were.

(Mrs) C. DAVIS

April 7th, 1954

PETTY DEGREES

SIR – In a famous case which has been occupying the public attention recently the prisoner is always spoken of as 'Dr' in the press. His degree is American, I presume. Are the quotation marks to show it is not English? If so, it is a most excellent practice, and ought to be followed in the case of all worthless degrees, especially if honorary, coming from the other side of the Herring Pond. Unfortunately the English pulpit is disgraced by them.

A few years ago 'The Christian World' fought the scandal in the Law Courts, and a few of the culprits moulted their gorgeous plumage. The practice is being revived; petty schools are conferring absurd degrees... Then as to the wearing of hoods. There are no American D.D. hoods; nevertheless some with the honorary degree from petty schools wear what is neither more nor les than the Oxford LL.D. hood...

> **C.C.**
>
> September 2nd, 1910

DISGRACEFUL ADULTS

SIR – I notice, with interest, that there is going to be a three-month road safety campaign for children. As a mother of two children, I am all in favour of it – but I do wish some one would organise one for the grown-ups! I think their behaviour on the crossings in this town is absolutely disgraceful.

At the end of the Pantiles we have lights and my small daughter has been taught that she must not cross until 'the writing shows.' But how often do the older people wait for that? They dash in front of cars – no time or thought for the children who naturally think they can do the same. Many a time my children have said 'That lady went on the red light, why could we not go too?'

I think we ought to have a safety week for all –

any more of your readers agree? And if the police could co-operate, a severe reprimanding at least for all offenders.

A THOROUGH READER

July 14th, 1954

NO RESPECT FOR THE DEAD

SIR – I fully agree with what 'ex-Private' and 'One Who Came Back' say about the want of respect shown at the War Memorial. I pass it once or twice a day, and have not once seen a man raise his hat in passing, except my husband, who had remarked before anyone wrote of it in your paper that he thought it was the least those who, like himself, had lived to come home could do in honour of those who died for us.

SYLVIA NEWGASS

50, Woodbury Park Road

February 23rd, 1923

UNFORTUNATE GERMANS

SIR – Your correspondent on this subject has evaded the point which I understood to be conveyed by your note on the postponed performance of Brahm's *Deutsches Requiem*. No enlightened person would suggest that the music of everyone who had the misfortune to be born in Germany should be banished from the concert hall, in spite of the fact that the unspeakable Hun by his outrages against artistic as well as moral sentiment has made us loathe

95

everything German; nor would they quarrel with the use of Handel's triumphal and funereal marches at appropriate times…

> Yours faithfully,
> **'A TIME TO EVERY PURPOSE'**
> June 15th, 1918

MISERABLE FANCIERS

SIR – On behalf of the Committee of the Fanciers' Association, I beg to thank you for the very excellent report of our Show last week. It is a matter of considerable surprise that such a magnificent response by the Fancy all over the country to our efforts to place the Royal Borough in the foremost rank of provincial Shows should meet with such miserable support from the public in the town itself, the attendance on both days being so small that a large deficit will be created in the Association's funds, penning and Judges' fees being exceptionally heavy. Again thanking you.

> **HARRY G. WHIBLEY**
> Hon. Secretary
> 58, Beulah Road
> January 14th, 1912

If Only...

There are things in life that are so glaringly obvious that it is surprising that no one else sees them. What better way to discharge one's public duty and enlighten everyone that with a letter spelling out what they overlooked to date.

A BABY BRICKBAT

SIR – Having read your recent article on having a baby at Pembury Hospital, I have to come to the conclusion that there are few places where I should less like to have a baby, the reasons being:

1. No matter what fancy names may be given to having a baby and all about it, one can't alter childbirth.

2. The 10 days in hospital after the baby is born is about the only bit of peace one can bank on for the next few years, regardless of how good the baby is.

3. New-born babies are seldom a pretty sight and the thought of having to view not only one's own offspring but several other people's also for the duration of one's spell in the place finishes me.

A MOTHER
May 9th, 1952

A MODEST PROPOSAL

SIR – I cannot resist the impulse to say a word on this serious matter trusting, to your kindness to publish it. What work of real value can be formed for the unemployed? Our eastern coast gives (to me at all events), an emphatic answer, thus, 'Save us, and begin at once, and save us by the labour of the unemployed. Build us a long line of seawall, or breakwater.' It is a big thing, but quite practicable in these days. 'Save us from further destruction, from the voracious sea, and

98

in saving us, you may save thousands of human lives, from starvation, desperation, and destruction.' It will prove a paying invest in the long run. Shall this urgent appeal from our wasting coasts be made in vain?

(Mrs) MARIA LANDER

November 21st, 1905

ROYAL GUINEA PIG

SIR – It is stated in the official account of his late Majesty's illness that 'he had received some months previously a vaccination treatment which it was hoped would secure him for some time from catarrhal attacks;' but at least two subsequent attacks occurred, the last of which proved fatal. Is it not advisable that the public should know exactly the nature of the inoculation treatment, since it evidently proved a failure? The nation's loss cannot be repaired, but others might avoid similar inoculation as being, to say the least, useless.

BEATRICE E. KIDD

Secretary, British Union for the Abolition of Vivisection.

May 13th, 1910

UNGRATEFUL MANDARIN

SIR – As one of those present at the opening ceremony of the Technical Institute, held last Tuesday at the Opera House, I was greatly surprised to hear no reference whatever to the handsome and valuable present just made by Mr C. Tattershall Dodd of the two copper plates which grace the entrance of the Institute on either side; and all the more, since these artistic additions to the beauty of the building, involving as they did an immense amount of skilful labour in their production, are entirely the work of Mr Dodd's own hands.

It was also remarkable that the Mayor, in thanking various gentlemen for their efforts in connection with the Institute, made no allusion to the unremitting and quite exceptional work which Mr George Abbott as devoted to the cause of technical education in this town, from the earliest days to the present time.

Yours truly
ASTONISHED
November 7th, 1902

GRAVE ERRORS

SIR – I should like to ask what right certain individuals have to cut down trees off graves in Southborough Churchyard without asking permission of the owners of such graves? It seems to me as if a certain few think they can do what they like, and no one will take any notice of them. I suppose if I went on their property and cut even a stick I should at once be prosecuted. If they had asked for the tree to be removed I daresay it would have been done.

But no, they like to think they are rulers, I suppose. If such things as trees are an eyesore to them perhaps they will kindly buy a burying ground where people can bury their dead free, and then, perhaps, they will be able to have what they like in it.

100

I think it is time steps were taken to put a stop to such things.

AN OFFENDED PARTY

April 27th, 1900

DRAUGHTY PITS

SIR – If you can give me a few lines in your paper I shall be much obliged if you will allow me to complain of the draught in the Opera House. This appears to be far worse in the pit than elsewhere, and is sometimes very unpleasant. The reason seems to be owning to the inside doors being left open as well as the outside, which really does not seem to be at all necessary, as most of the people take their seats before the performance commences. As this part of the building holds more people than elsewhere, surely something ought to be done to make it more comfortable? I am not the only one to complain, as I have overheard others.

A FREQUENT 'PIT-GOER'

May 22nd, 1903

PROPER SPELLING BLOW UP

SIR – Letter writing in my present abode is a rather difficult matter; the climate being warm, ink dries, and paper gets scorched, but we manage it somehow, and also it is a task to write in modern English.

Newspapers, especially bad ones, are not allowed, but good papers get through occasionally. I read in the *Advertiser* of last week the saying of one Fooks.

Is not this name a relative of mine? If so, he ought to spell his name correctly. Why Fooks? – Is he ashamed of Fawkes, a good old historic name, remembered every 5th of November? But Fooks. Faugh! Phoo-x! I can't bear it! You say Phoo-x is a Conservative. I am ashamed of him. Now, I was a reformer, a Radical root-and-branch man, to make an end of the lot – King, Lords and Commons – and I nearly succeeded, too. From his talk, I should judge this Fooks to be a lawyer. I can't abide lawyers – they get it hot here. A lawyer fellow named Coke was at my trial. He is now shovelling red-hot coke a few stages lower down. This Fooks has, I see, been speaking strangely of the people in office, and of their want of money (that's in bad taste), and of their uncles (that's vulgar), and of loyal Ulstermen, who, I am told, want to go on rebellion and murder Papists – in fact, he let off gas enough to fill our big hall. Well, I fear I must disown Fooks.

If he is a Catholic he ought to take a cooling drink, and go to see his confessor. Wild and rash talk approaching unto calumny, and bearing false witness are matters for confession, I suppose, and I think there are nine ways or so of being accessory to another person's sin, and a person (even poor 'Phoo-x') may be guilty of a lot of these ways.... But really he ought to spell his name correctly, as does

> Yours very warmly,
> **GUY FAWKES**
> The Shades,
> February 3rd, 1912

SCARRED WORDS

SIR – After your welcome publicity concerning the thefts and mutilation of books from the Public Library, I think it is an opportune moment to mention the widespread pencil-marking and annotation of Public Library books also going on, especially among the non-fiction stock.

Unfortunately there are certain members of the public who are so selfish that they do not trouble to consider the annoyance caused to subsequent readers by their unwelcome, and often stupid, remarks in the margins. Other people wish to read the book with an open mind, and to consider the author's views for themselves, without being distracted and irritated by the opinions of others.

As it is rarely possible for the library staff to detect the offender, this underhand practice is all the more deplorable, and, to anyone who has any consideration for others, quite inexplicable.

NORAH M. BARTLETT

May 14th, 1943

SUMMERY DESECRATION

SIR – As a frequent visitor to Tonbridge and Tunbridge Wells, I never fail to feel a sense of exhilaration at the beautiful views obtained from the tops of buses.

One, particularly, is that seen on the run from Southborough to Tonbridge, with the checkerboard pattern of the Weald of Kent on the one side and well-wooded parts of Sussex in the distance on the other.

What a pity it is that in the spring and summer the people of these towns (or could it be mainly the visitors?) leave so much ugly litter about at such places as Tunbridge Wells Common, the Calverley Grounds and in the streets.

During the war there were anti-litter regulations and sometimes prosecutions under them. I would like to see them enforced again, for I dislike intensely the prospect of seeing ice-cream wrappers and tubs (to name only one type of nuisance) desecrating the beautiful green swards.

Could you not invite readers to submit some anti-litter slogans on the lines of the road safety slogans you now publish? As an example, I suggest: 'Take your rubbish with you; don't leave it on the pavement or grass.' But plenty of readers could coin better phrases than this – it is only a suggestion.

Why not make this a 'Clean Summer' year in Tonbridge and Tunbridge Wells?

CONSTANT VISITOR
March 3rd, 1954

APPALLING PLASTER

SIR – As a frequent visitor to Tunbridge Wells – and visitors are an important item in the welfare of the town – I crave your indulgence to protest against the unsightly exhibition with which a house at the end of Beltring Road had been plastered. One has, alas! learnt to expect such nuisances in the meaner localities in London, but one certainly looks for some escape from glaring placards in this charming health resort. To find a respectable residential thoroughfare suddenly reduced to the level of an East-End slum is exasperating, not only to visitors, but also to residents, and one wonders if the person who is responsible for the outrage is in any way interested in the value of the property, and, if so, whether he has weighed the trifling advantage he expects to gain now with his losses in the future. It is a well-known fact that once property of this kind is started on the downward grade the most superlative efforts fail, more often than not, to stop the rot. Not so long ago every house in Beltring Road was let; now there are four 'To Let' notice boards to be seen, and I am not surprised to hear of further migrations in the near future.

COMMONWEAL

June 12th, 1903

A CAPITAL IDEA

SIR – It would probably be a source of much enjoyment to our visitors and also residents if they could be allowed to view the extensive and unrivalled scenery from the top of Rusthall Church bell tower, which, might also become a source of income in the same way as at St. Paul's Cathedral.

F.G.

April 24th, 1912

NUMBERS UP

SIR – There are some 1,800 named houses in Tunbridge Wells. The names are occasionally changed, and in some cases the same name is borne by more than one house. What an amount of labour in letter and parcel sorting must this involve? Let us, therefore, in these high-pressure times, still use – if so we wish – the name of a house, but give also the street name and street number.

A RESIDENT

July 13th, 1917

TOO MUCH COUGHING AND SPITTING

SIR – The time is not far distant when visitors and intending residents will ask: 'Is there a stringent bye-law against spitting in public places?' as regularly as they now enquire whether the town is drained and kept and watched as it should be.

May I correct one popular misapprehension? The presence in a town of consumptives who know they are affected and who have been, or are, under treatment is no menace to public health. These people know full well the dangers of infection, and would no sooner think of spitting in the street or any public place than would a medical man.

The real danger proceeds from the numbers who have this disease, but who are ignorant that they are infected, and that they can infect others. Such people, through sheer ignorance, may make consumptives of healthy people, though they themselves may have the good fortune to throw off the disease by reason of their own vitality. Against this danger it is the duty of the town authority to protect us by an anti-spitting bye-law.

WEEK-END VISITOR
June 19th, 1903

PICK MORE FLOWERS

SIR – One thing has struck me ever since I resided in Tunbridge Wells: Why, in this 'Garden of England' do we not have a flower show? Do not people love flowers in Kent? Do not they grow them? And would they not, if they had the chance, come and see them?

W. WEARING
Brampton Rise
January 16th, 1922

NO MORE BURYING ALIVE

SIR – As I believe many people are afraid of being buried alive, will you allow me, through the columns of your paper, to call the attention of your readers to the Society of Premature Burial, the existence of which many of them may not be aware of?

Full particulars of its methods and aims will be supplied gratis on application to Mr H. Denton Ingham, 12, London-street, London, E.C.

A SUBSCRIBER
May 26th, 1905

RUBBISH FILMS

SIR – The motion picture industry, terrified by TV, is turning to giant screens, trick sound systems and 3-D in an attempt to fill the cinemas.

Will it succeed? I doubt it. For if some of the puerile second features seen locally in recent months had been in 3-D on a screen as big as the back of the Assembly Hall they still wouldn't have appealed to me.

Yet the answer to the cinema industry's TV phobia is as plain as a pikestaff. Let us have more films like 'The Cruel Sea,' 'Malta Story,' 'Sound Barrier' and 'Genevieve,' to name a few that have been shown in Tunbridge Wells picture theatres this year. I noticed no empty seats then.

Isn't the position simply this, TV programmes, with some exceptions, are of a rather low entertainment standard. But the novelty value of TV at the present time gains these programmes an audience. Cinemas were filled before TV's advent even though shows were frequently indifferent. People simply went there in order to 'fill-in' an empty evening – and this function is now performed by TV Hence the empty cinemas unless a really worthwhile film is being screened.

Let the cinema give us good films. I would far sooner have one main feature, plus a couple of short documentaries, than spend 90 minutes of misery watching a fifth-rate second feature that would insult the lowliest intelligence.

S.H. MARSHALL

September 23rd, 1953

TOO MANY AMATEUR ACTORS

SIR – Your columnist writing in 'A Seat in the Stalls' last week has hit the nail right on the head when he says that there are far too many amateur dramatic societies in Tunbridge Wells. It is a fact that has been painfully obvious for some time.

I do not think the public is entirely to blame for the state of apathy that exists either. Most of the plays that our societies put on are either well-tried recent London successes (I can think of at least two performed within the last three months) or hackneyed pieces which most repertory companies can stage at the drop of a hat.

Let our societies pool their resources by all means. But let them have the courage to tackle something out of the ordinary – something with a large cast and plenty of scene-changes and something above all with a damn good plot.

There are many plays in this category simply lying idle because no one has the temerity to take them on. (Priestley's 'Good Companions' and 'Johnson over Jordan' are cases in point.) We have good amateur actors and producers in our midst. Let them put their heads together.

Since I am a member of one of the societies concerned I should prefer it to be thought that I have no axe to grind either and so I sign myself.

PLAYGOER

June 2nd, 1954

109

STIRRING WORDS

SIR – From the correspondence your columnist has stirred up over the number of amateur dramatic societies in this town, it would appear that there is not quite so much apathy towards the theatre as he supposes.

This is a very good sign, and I hope my own comments will not be superfluous.

'Playgoer's' remarks on the type of play we put on may be at first reading seem to have some justice, but when you come to think of it, isn't it rather difficult to find a play that has not been a success in London?

By that I mean, of course, a worthwhile play. As to the 'hackneyed pieces,' I would be the first to admit that The Importance of Being Earnest might come in that category but the lines are as fresh today as they were 60 years ago. I hope 'Playgoer' will grace us with his presence on The Pantiles next week, in spite of his feelings.

Again, I must agree with a comparison with 'drawing-room charades', but only up to a point.

I have always held the opinion that no-one enjoys an amateur performance as much as the actors themselves. And surely that very feeling of enjoyment can, and does, reach across the footlights and infect the audience? By all means let us cut out the charade attitude towards drama, but amateur acting is a hobby and a hobby should be fun.

DAVID MAITLAND

June 9th, 1954

Please Note

Little is wrong with Tunbridge Wells, evidently. But since you ask, there are a few small improvements that can be made...

BODY BLOWS

SIR – Mr Dodwell calls attention to an important question, and I earnestly hope that his appeal for the welding together of the Tunbridge Wells anti-vaccinators into a branch of the National Anti-Vaccination League may be immediately responded to. Some encouragement for a determined and bold policy of 'no surrender' may be found in the recent declaration of the heterogeneous body the Imperial Vaccination League, 'The abolition of 'conscientious objector' will not be urged.'

Of course not. This is quite too kind an admission, and really all conscientious objectors ought to be profoundly thankful for such conde-scension, and but for the fact that we have nothing to be thankful to this imperial body for, we should be under deep and lasting obligation. Now is your time, my anti-vaccination friends, to press home your righteous demands. Waver not: press forward, for the goal is well in sight. Falter not, and you may soon, plant the standard of victory on the citadel of your very own castle, out of which you have too long been ousted by the cunning and audacity of the enemy.

W.T. MARTIN

January 16th, 1903

HEALTH CASH COW

SIR – Mr J.R. Williamson's letter in your last issue touches incidentally upon the protective powers of vaccination against smallpox. Since that letter was

112

OUTRAGED OF TUNBRIDGE WELLS

written we have, thanks to the Imperial Vaccination League, further information. Jenner declared that one vaccination was absolute protection for life. And upon that idea our present law of compulsory vaccination for infants is based.

During the last half century the period of protection has been narrowed down first to ten years, then to seven years, and now to a qualified five years! Say the Imperial Vaccination League: – 'Vaccination in infancy, plus re-vaccination on going to school at five years of age, together with re-vaccination every time smallpox contact is known or suspected, will secure complete immunity.'

So in short, provided one is vaccinated and re-vaccinated, and takes care to keep away from smallpox infection, safety is assured!

Really, it would seem that the 'protective' power is being rapidly whittled down until very soon we shall require vaccinating every week! What a glorious harvest of seven-and-sixpences for the doctors!

G. R. DODWELL.

January 23rd, 1903

THE NEW STAR CHAMBER

SIR – I note that oppression is still rampant, and people are again forced to stand up manfully for their rights and liberties and form a new Anti-Vaccination Society to resist oppression and law breakers, who instead of acting like law abiding citizens, and in their capacity as Justices of the Peace, cause strife and ill-feeling, and say individually to honest men.

113

Poor short-sighted man, unmindful of the fact that 'As you sow, so will you reap.' One minister of religion (so-called) adds insult to injury by remarking that anti-vaccinators are an ignorant set of people. Thanks for the gospel of love and goodwill.

CONSCIENCE

July 31st, 1903

REWARD SHOT

SIR – May I take the liberty of asking you (in the interest of the public at large) to state through the medium of your valuable journal, the fact that all persons depositing hedge cuttings, broken glass, or rubbish of any description upon any public highway are liable to be prosecuted, and may be subjected under the Highway Act (1835) to a fine not exceeding 40s. and in addition any damage that may be caused thereby.

I may also add that the Cyclists' Touring Club, 47, Victoria-street, Westminster, are prepared to give a £2 reward for evidence that results in the conviction of the offender or offenders. Thanking you in anticipation.

CHARLES BEECHER

December 3rd, 1900

GIRL-SNATCHERS

SIR – Will you allow me, through the medium of your columns, to warn your readers against receiving into their houses the leaflets, 'Rays of Living Light,' that are now flooding the town.

They are being circulated by a sect now calling themselves 'The Church of Jesus Christ of Latter-day Saints,' but who are in reality Mormons, some of them missionaries over from America.

In Mormonism we have one of the most pernicious forms of infidelity and blasphemy and while professing to teach only the Gospel of Jesus Christ, they weave in most subtle form their doctrinal errors, while they keep in the background their 'Book of Mormon Doctrines and Covenants, etc.' Not only is their teaching erroneous, but seeking, as they do, to draw young girls over to Utah, they become a danger to women. And they may be seen and heard day after day in Tunbridge Wells talking with maid-servants at the doors, seeking to ensnare them.

Should anyone wish to confirm for themselves this warning, may I suggest that they communicate with Mr W.R. Bradlaugh, 70, King's-rad, London, E.C., who will freely give any information. He also supplies a leaflet, worthy of purchase, 'Mormon Infidelity and Polygamy,' post free, 1½d.

BEE

February 28th, 1908

WHO IS PAYING FOR THIS?

SIR – Recently I noticed a big lorry standing in the drive of a neighbouring requisitioned house.

On it was piled a large quantity of 'junk,' paper, wood, cardboard, etc., which two men were solemnly carrying to the garden at the back and depositing in what used to be the lawn.

One of them told me that it was to make a bonfire for the children, and that what appeared to be a revolving office chair, on top of everything, was for the 'Guy' to sit on!

Times have indeed changed. In my youth, one tramped long distances to obtain material for the same purpose, and saved up our pocket-money (mine was 1d. a week) to buy fireworks. Who pays?

G. FRASER SIMSON

November 18th, 1953

DOUBTFUL OLIVE

SIR – My attention has been called to a report in your last issue of a case heard before the Tonbridge Bench on the 4th, arising out of an alleged assault by a Mrs Damper, of Spring Hill Farm, Fordcombe, upon Mrs Alice Hollamby. As the report reflects seriously on me, I must ask you to allow me to explain that although I was passing by at the time, I took no part in the disturbance, and the statements reported to have been made by Mrs Damper and one of her witnesses that I in anyway interfered with Mrs Damper or urged any other person present to molest her, must be due to a mistaken identity.

OLIVE MARGARET FAUCHON

Waters Green, Penshurst
October 13th, 1910

BEWARE OF A FOREIGN INVASION

SIR – I desire to issue a serious warning to the public to be on their guard against accepting anything but the genuine poppies sold for the benefit of distressed ex-Servicemen and their dependants on Armistice Day. It is evident that preparations have been made – sometimes by foreign firms – to flood the streets and florists' shops with artificial poppies made solely for private gain...

HAIG, F.-M.

October 8th, 1926

GET RICH QUICK

SIR – I venture to prophesy that in a few years, when we live in the happy days of peace on earth and goodwill amongst all people, machines in the air will be as plentiful as bicycles on the road. They will be made to float in the air at a low altitude so that the most timorous body need not be afraid.

I had a dream the other night, and have since elaborated the idea. The 'Airette' will consist of a light boat attached to a cigar-shaped balloon inflated with gas or compressed air, which will raise the whole – including the controller – to about a foot from the earth. The petrol engine in the boat will be set in motion, and will drive the screw-propeller at the rear, or two paddle wheels at the sides. A fish tail will regulate the rise and fall of the machine to the desired altitude – for the timid a few feet and for the daring any height. To avoid collision with trees or chimney pots they might follow the main roads, as

117

do motor cars, but with the advantage of being able to float over the bushes out of the way of approaching danger. A parachute would be fixed on the balloon, which will gently lower the whole thing to earth in case of mishap to the propeller.

Now, as many millions of people in the world would be glad to avail themselves of so easy and pleasant a joy-ride, it follows that a great fortune awaits a company with capital, and who secure the patent. Amongst all my present personal friends, sir, you stand the highest, and I freely take you into my secret in order that you may share the profit. The only condition is that you find a competent and enterprising engineer to work out the details. There must be many in Manchester.

The size of the balloon would of course be regulated by the weight to lift. No doubt stations would be available in most districts to supply gas or compressed air. I submit this dream to you for criticism and suggestion, and shall anxiously await your reply. I seem to feel the shadow of Mr H.G. Wells hovering over me, and denouncing my presumption in trespassing in his domain.

Yours faithfully,
CHARLES CRABTREE
14, Guildford Street
August 30th, 1917

[*We are overwhelmed with the possibility of our prospective wealth. When we come across an engineer in Manchester willing to be Mr Crabtree's collaborator we will send him a 'wireless.' — Ed.*]

CERTAINLY NOT ME

SIR – I was greatly surprised to find a letter in last week's paper giving my address and signed in my name. I beg to say I had nothing whatever to do with this letter; neither have I the slightest idea as to what person had the audacity to publish such a letter in my name. Hoping you will kindly insert this in your next week's paper.

Yours faithfully,

T. HICKS

57, Colebrook Road

May 4th, 1927

RECORD EGG

SIR – One of my Rhode Island hens laid an egg measuring 8 ½ inches round lengthways, 6in diameter, weight 5 ½ ozs, containing three distinct yolks.

(Mrs) G. GARRETT

70, Goods Station Road

March 14th, 1924

JAZZED UP

SIR – I wonder if you would be good enough to spare a few lines of your valuable space to give publicity to a new club which is being formed in Tunbridge Wells. This takes the form of a 'Rhythm Club' – a club devoted to the interests of lovers of modern rhythmic music.

The idea of the club is to enable members to get together, say, once a week, to listen to all the best of the latest records issued by Gramophone Companies of such well-known coloured 'stars' as Ellington, Henderson, Hawkins, Armstrong, etc., and the band of our own Lew Stone, all acknowledged to be the leading exponents of modern rhythm. There are a number of these clubs all over the country, and they are greatly appreciated by all young people, and especially by local dance musicians.

If any of your readers are interested, I should be pleased to let them have further particulars.

NEVILL P. YOUNG

Acting Secretary
152, Camden Road
September 21st, 1934

GROOVY

SIR – With reference to my recent letter re the above club, I should like to thank you for publishing the same in your paper.

I have had numerous replies in response to it, with the result that we have been able to arrange our first meeting, which will include a recital of 'hot' records, for Friday evening next (28th September) at 8 p.m. at the Mikado Café, 9, Vale Road, Tunbridge Wells.

Prospective members are cordially invited to come along. Again thanking you

NEVILL P. YOUNG, Hon. Secretary

September 28th, 1934

THE BEST GIRLS

SIR – I am writing on behalf of two other chaps in the mess as well as myself; they are: Donald Yates (E.M) and Eric Cousins (R.G.M.), both of the same address as myself.

We would appreciate it very much if you would put a couple of lines in your newspaper about us, as we would like some pen-friends of the opposite sex from up there. We will be able to come up and see them sometimes when we are in dock as it is not a very long way from Portsmouth. We are aged as follows: Eric is 20, Don is 19 and I am 18.

The reason we have picked Tunbridge Wells is that we have heard a lot from a chap in our mess by name of Brough, who lives at The Royal Oak, Tonbridge. He says they are the best girls in Britain so naturally we have taken him up on that.

> **GEORGE J. HUSBANDS**
> H.M.S *Vigo*, c/o F.M.O. Portsmouth
> November 10th, 1954

SILENT NIGHTS

SIR – It came as more than a surprise to my mess-mates and myself that the challenge issued to the young womanhood of your town has been taken so seriously. We have never had so many letters on the mess deck in one day before, except once, when during Operation Mariner, of September last year, the mail was delayed for three weeks.

121

A point of interest though, is the fact that the whole thing was done on the spur of the moment. I, like the majority, am a non-participant, but we all shared the 'discomfort' of the three instigators.

They never really expected any form of reply, so the girls of Tunbridge Wells have given them something to think about, especially those who enclosed photographs. This evening, at the time of writing, the mess is under a pall of quietude never before experienced. The lads are deeply engrossed in concocting suitable replies to their respective pen-pals.

The reason for this letter is to acknowledge my thanks to you and your paper for indirectly bringing a little peace to this ship. I will remain eternally grateful for this heavenly peace.

Yours sincerely,

PETER WHELAMS

H.M.S. *Vigo*, c/o F.M.O. Portsmouth

November 17th, 1954

Kind Hearts

Although perhaps less vocal than others, Tunbridge Wells does have inhabitants who consider their fellow men as glasses who are half-full rather than half-empty, and who can be prevailed upon.

COMFORT CALL

SIR – It is the bounden duty of every humane person to help those who cannot help themselves. Surely if the officials in asylums are highly remunerated, the patients ought to receive more comforts and better food. Our asylums system requires thorough overhauling. People of all shades of political opinion see eye to eye on this important question. I am sure in a town like Tunbridge Wells this measure, when brought in, would receive the hearty support of the people of your town.

VOX POPULI VOX DEI

April 19th, 1912

CROWNING EFFORT

SIR – Your account of the meeting re celebration of the Coronation, makes interesting reading, in the enthusiasm displayed by the various speakers when airing their pet schemes to make the event a success, but there was one class of men who do not appear to be represented at that meeting, who probably would have been able to have given the Committee an idea that never appeared to strike those present.

I mean the working men who will have to sacrifice two and perhaps three days' wages on account of their works being closed for that time.

If I might be allowed to make a suggestion, it is this, that before any of the ratepayers' £500 is thrown away in the provision of decorations and senseless perambulation of the streets, a portion should be set aside for the purpose of compensating those workers who are compelled to remain idle during all the junketing. If this is not done I am afraid there will be a big skeleton at the feast, and to me at least a feeling of distress would prevail at the knowledge that those who can least afford it, are called upon to make so heavy a sacrifice for such small returns.

A COMPOUND RATEPAYER

April 25th, 1902

SWEEPING ASIDE

SIR – This wet winter has been particularly hard on a class of men who are never sufficiently well paid for their labour to enable them to lay by much for a rainy day. I refer to the jobbing gardeners.

An instance of want of consideration towards them has come to my notice this week, which I think only needs mentioning to be remedied. A young and energetic gardener went round each morning on Monday, Tuesday, Wednesday to sweep the snow from his own clients' drives and doorsteps. As he was in their – more or less regular – employ, he did not feel entitled to ask for remuneration and in only one case was it offered him.

As he gave this useful service to 36 or 37 houses each day, a payment of 2d. each would have left him with a good day's wage in his pocket for which he had certainly given a good day's work. As it was he returned home each day with only 6d. to show for his many hours' work. If he had neglected his employers, and gone to the houses of strangers, he

125

would, without doubt, have been better off.

I hope if this letter comes to their eyes, each of this man's employers will feel that they owe him a least 6d.

THE ONE WHO PAID

March 4th, 1904

JUSTICE CHECKED

SIR – 'Justitia' has, apparently, a great reverence for the cash nexus between man and man. Personally, with my fellow Socialists, I don't consider that a man's relations to his fellows should be placed on such a narrow basis. Try thinking of Milton writing 'Paradise Lost' at so much a line, or Saint Paul being paid a salary of £300, or even £1,000 a year for preaching. You can't do it…

FILIUS NULLIUS

January 19th, 1900

CHARITY NONSENSE

SIR – After considerable difficulty in many ways, I succeeded in getting an able-bodied man and his family of six children out of the workhouse, where they had been a burden on the rates for seven or eight years, the wife of the man having been in a lunatic asylum for eight years, and applied to the Charity Organisation Society for a little help to enable the man (who had obtained a situation at a farm where he had worked 15 years before, and for the same master), to produce a few articles of furniture and bedding, as he literally had nothing except a few things given to him out of charity. I was closely questioned on many points as to the man's respectability, and also his wife's, the ages and names of each of the children, etc., to which I had some difficulty obtaining. The Charity Organisation Society allowed it to be a most deserving and distressing case, but after gaining all the information they required, and going a few days after for the help I fully expected, was told, 'That as it was just outside their boundary, they could do nothing.' This is only one of the many instances I have known of the inquisitiveness and uselessness of the Charity Organisation Society.

A LOVER OF JUSTICE

January 9th, 1900

INDECENT EXPOSURE

SIR – Although it is well known that young men and boys in the Navy are liable to severe floggings with the cane and birch, many people imagine that the 'cat' has been abandoned. A 'cat' is carried on every ship, though it cannot be used, but as Mr Tighe Hopkins points out in the *Law Times* a man can be sent to prison and flogged 'for the maintenance of disciplines a method of procedure which looks very like an evasion of the law.' It must be admitted that we are the best men in the Navy we can get, but how are the best, most eligible recruits, to be obtained by the Admiralty if young men are made aware that, for simply smoking or not swimming a required distance, they are liable to be indecently exposed, slung over a gun, and flogged in the presence of their assembled shipmates?

It is supposed that England and Russia are the only civilized powers that retain this loathsome and gruesome relic of barbarism, and whilst certain English Admirals have recently been searching the Scriptures for vestiges of an argument in its support, reports have it that the Czar even now abolished flogging in the Russian Navy. We were almost the last to abolish flogging in the Army, and it seems – to show our 'divine destiny' as the greatest civilizing power – we are to be the last to abandon flogging in the Navy.

ARCHIBALD WEBB PEPLOE

September 23rd, 1904

DOZING MAGISTRATES

SIR – On reading the columns of your issue of February 22nd I was struck by the reports of two cases which were tried in the local Police Courts. One was headed, 'Stolen Diamond Pin.' If the evidence as reported by you is correct, the case against the boy should have been dismissed, on the ground that the prosecutor 'offered an inducement to the prisoner to confess his guilt.' This is against the law. I was recently in a London Police Court, where a case was being heard. Exactly the same inducement (*i.e.*, forgiveness) was offered by the prosecutor to the prisoner. On hearing this evidence, the presiding Magistrate immediately stopped the case, and though the prisoner had pleaded guilty, the case was dismissed. Where was the Magistrate's Clerk?

Case No. 2 – horse cruelty. This was tried at Tonbridge. Two men were charged, one with 'working' and the other 'with causing to be worked,' a horse in an unfit state. The R.S.P.C.A. Inspector, in his evidence – which, by the way was not backed up by a veterinary surgeon's, though there was one in Court who was called for a later cruelty case – said that 'the sores could not have been in the state he found them in 48 hours.'

In spite of expert evidence given in their favour, one defendant was found guilty and fined, but the other acquitted. Now, sir, as the sores (if any) were 'more than 48 hours forming,' the foreman who sent the horse to work was as equally guilty or not guilty as the man who worked the horse. The case never ought to have been brought.

INTERESTED

March 1st, 1907

BARE FEET

SIR – I wish to acknowledge with many thanks the receipt of 10s. 6d. from 'Reu' for the purpose of providing boots for some of the very poor boys of the school. I have already expended the money, and there are still many whose feet are partly bare, and I should be very thankful to receive any further small donations for the same purpose. We should

be glad to receive second-hand boots.
CHAS. M. MALPASS
January 14th, 1910

HAND MAIDENS

SIR – During the war there has naturally been a great shortage of domestic servants, hundreds of girls leaving their work for the more important work of their country. The time has now come when mistresses expect maids to return, but will they ever return under the same conditions as before? Practically all have the same grievance – lack of outings. Much has been done during the war for girls in other branches of life, simply because there is a Committee or Union at the head of them. Why cannot something similar be done for domestic servants?

Mistresses would find that they would benefit equally as much as the maid. Competition would once more start, and mistresses be able to pick and choose, thereby gaining a far better class servant, instead of continuing, as in lots of instances lately, where the 'Maid is the Mistress of the Situation.'
THREE OF 'EM
December 13th, 1918

LADY POWER

SIR – Might I suggest to some of our Tunbridge Wells ladies, now that their strenuous labours in connection with the war are over, that they might be doing a national, and a local service, by forming a Ladies' Guild in Tunbridge Wells for the betterment of maid servants. At present it is chaos, thanks largely to the Government's badly managed out-of-work payments.

It is said that a thousand servants are wanted in Tunbridge Wells, and yet scores of domestic servants are doing nothing. I counted 300 advertisements in *The Times* recently for servants. Every sensible mistress realises that girls in this class of work will not go on as before the war.

The pay must be higher, the hours shorter, and other considerations. Most mistresses are ready to make these concessions and for the sake of mistress and maid I suggest the ladies should form such a guild and draw up a scale of pay, hours of work, holidays, etc., etc., so that a united scheme might be launched satisfactory to both sides. Both mistress and maid might be encouraged to join such a guild, each knowing what to expect.

If a few ladies could meet and just set this going, they would be conferring a great blessing on a large number.

CITIZEN
May 30th, 1919

HEARTLESS DISLOYALTY

SIR – One would prefer at this season of peace and goodwill to refrain from grumbling, but in the light of our good King's recent command that Tuesday, the 27th, should be kept as a Bank Holiday, it seems very hard and indeed disloyal, that, our Borough employees should for some reason or other, have been compelled to work on that date. When one considers that the monotonous and (under some conditions) the extremely depressing nature of the work in which our dustmen and road sweepers are engaged, one would think that of all men an extra day's holiday would prove most beneficial to these.

A SYMPATHISER

December 28th, 1910

War

The war brings out the best and worst in people and Tunbridge Wells is certainly no exception. Behind the stiff upper lip, passions boil – most certainly where the Home Guard is involved.

World War I

GERMANS EXACTLY

SIR – A few days before the outbreak of the war an Englishman sitting in a café in Berlin was overheard by a German officer to allude to 'that d– – d fool of an Emperor.' He was immediately arrested for *lèse majesté*, and taken before the Burgomaster. The Englishman pleaded in defence that he was alluding to the Emperor Austria. 'Come, come,' said the Magistrate, 'that won't do; everybody knows there is only one d– – d fool of an Emperor, that is the Kaiser.'

J.M.

August 21st, 1914

PETTICOAT FOLLY

SIR – As one who volunteered when war commenced and was rejected, and is now again trying to enlist, I write to protest against the foolish posters now being put out in the town, headed, 'Wanted Petticoats.' I do not know who is responsible for them, whether man or woman, though I am inclined to the latter, but I would like to point out: –

i) That it is quite the wrong way to obtain recruits by trying to insult the young men we need and by appealing to their baser instincts.

ii) That the right and only way is for the author of the posters to speak to and appeal to the sense of honour and duty of every young man he or she

134

meets, explaining the causes of the war, the country's need, and the terms of enlistment. By this means we shall obtain the men we need.

In conclusion, I would say that my hope is that we shall shortly see women taking the place of men in all shops, omnibuses, etc., and every able-bodied man in the ranks. White feathers and talk of petticoats will be a hindrance rather than a help to this end, and I trust that we shall see and hear no more of this childish folly in Tunbridge Wells.

> **J. YULE ELLIOT**
> September 2nd, 1914

GERMAN-SPY THREAT

SIR – I am informed that in some hotels, etc., in this town there are German employees. I suggest, therefore, that you should publish a list of hotels whose proprietors, or managers, are able to state, 'British only employed.' Let us hope the others will come into line, and discharge Germans....

> **J.W. MARSDIN NEWTON**
> September 2nd, 1914

INCONSIDERATE LIGHTS

SIR – Taking a walk round the town on the night of the 10th inst., I was much surprised to notice how very thoughtless many people are, the greatest offenders being the trades people , especially certain publicans (these have a special licence) with strong shafts of light emanating from the premises, which could be seen by a Zeppelin for miles. Then there are the motor cars of the rich, with their glaring headlights... Again there is a woman with a flashlight, a thing that ought to be put a stop to, and at once....

ONE WHO SUFFERED IN A RAID
November 12th, 1915

WARMING JACKETS

SIR – Will you give me room to name to your readers a scheme I have had in working since early October? I undertake to dye khaki any sweaters sent me for the troops, and to forward them to the proper quarter. I have already distributed 11,400 sent me from all parts of the world... When sweaters are not to be at hand, I can make good use of ladies' golf jackets – any colour and form except the very short and much-shaped type. Out of a lady's golf coat I can make a khaki vest, a muffler and mits...

JOHN PENOYRE
February 8th, 1915

FIGHTING GLOVES

SIR – I have been asked to collect gifts of all kinds or suede gloves to be made into waistcoats for soldiers and sailors fighting on land and sea....

(Mrs) GERTRUDE WEARING
October 1st, 1915

MOUTH ORGANS

SIR – Just a few lines to ask you if you will try and do us a kindness. Would you ask some of your readers if they could manage to send us a couple of mouth-organs, so that we can have a little tune up when we get behind the firing line, as we find it monotonous? I am a native of Tunbridge Wells...

PTE G. PEARSON, 2439

January 28th, 1916

CRUCIFICATION SOVEREIGNS

SIR – To understand what a million really means is beyond the power of most people. Bearing this in mind, I have worked out the time needed to reach the amount of the recent War Loan, reckoning one sovereign for each minutes, with the result that to total £1,000,312,950 would require no less than 1,901 years, 48 weeks, 4 days and 18 ½ hours.

It therefore follows that if one sovereign had been laid aside each minute that has elapsed since our Lord was crucified the total would not yet have reached the huge amount which has been contributed to what we all much hope will prove to be the 'Victory Loan.'

H.M. CALEY

Cranwell House, Rusthall
March 9th, 1917

BLIGHTERS ON AN ISLAND

137

SIR – You are a war crank – shall I say fiend – for you care not how many hundreds of thousands of your countrymen are sacrificed, how much misery, how many wrecked homes, so long as your thirst for blood is unappeased. Talk about posterity, indeed. What will it be like, with unfit mothers, debilitated fathers, weighed down by a crushing load of taxation and dear food? No, sire, anything in the nature of an honourable peace is far better than this horrible conflict, which is a disgrace to humanity, and is only kept going by the comfortably placed to meet their own selfish ends. If only the politicians, rulers and newspaper editors could be shipped off to some uninhabited island in the South Pacific, there to fight it out among themselves, how much better the world would be without them. Anyway, I would put all such blighters as you in the trenches for two or three months. The survivor would probably be found with their war enthusiasm damped down.

DISSENTER

December 28th, 1917

[*It is not our policy to insert anonymous letters, but we really must make an exception in this case. – Ed.*]

World War II

FASCIST APPEAL

SIR – I feel sure that the readers of such a patriotic paper as yours must have observed with much concern the continual activities of Red

Revolutionaries in this country, and I should therefore be very glad if you would insert this letter in your columns, so that those who wish, in however small a way – to put another nail in the Communist coffin – may have an opportunity of doing so.

Your readers are probably aware that there are a very large number of Communist Sunday Schools existing in England to-day and that in these schools little children are taught to hate God, to despise all honour and morality and to live and to work only for the Red Revolution. In order to combat the evils of this teaching we have started a special fund for the purpose of organising Fascist Clubs for Children, and these have already been started with great success in a number of districts. Here the children are taught to love God, honour the King, and work for the good of their country.

I would point out that the children of to-day are the men and women of to-morrow, and I would invite all those who care for the future of the British Empire to send me a subscription, however small, towards this fund. Cheques should be cross, 'Fascist Clubs for Children,' and sent to me at our headquarters, Sussex Shades, Nevill-street, Tunbridge Wells.

(Mrs) ROSE STEWART
District Officer, Women's Units
October 16th, 1925

WHITE SLAVERY

SIR – Congratulations to Mr R.E. Martyr on his manly exposure of the diabolical plot to bring about

139

OUTRAGED OF TUNBRIDGE WELLS

the downfall of Britain and her Empire.

As one who has travelled extensively and lived for many years in distant parts of the Empire, it will interest your readers to know that the League of Nations is invariably known as the League of Jews; and though it may be sponsored by certain brands of peer, pacifist parsons and lawyers who command and demand fat fees., it is the willing, or, possibly unwilling, too of International Jewry, as was publicly stated by the late Walter Rathenau when he was head of A.E.G. and the most powerful Jew in Europe.

No decent citizen objects to the League of Nations, but what he does object to is Britain and her Colonies being governed by such insignificant states as Guatemala and Liberia, and all the time knowing that the power behind it all is the International Jew, for whom, according to Mr Passmore's list, large numbers of so-called 'Leading People' are so ardently working.

For more people would believe in the League of Nations it is would only concentrate its attention on the horrors of traffic in women, known as the White Slave Traffic which, according to the Jew press, is practically a Jew monopoly....

BRITON

August 28th, 1931

ITALIAN PERFIDY

SIR – In view of the energy with which the British Union of Fascists have defended Mussolini's Abyssinian aggression, it would be interesting to learn how they can reconcile that policy with the following speech which was delivered by Mussolini at Rome on December 30th 1936.

'How can it be thought,' said he, only five short years ago, 'that I consider without horror the eventuality of war? To-day a war, even if it broke out between two nations only, would become fatally universal, and the whole of civilisation would be in danger. Italy will never take the initiative in a war. She needs peace. Fascism seeks to assure to the Italian people a future of prosperity and peace.'

C. CLAXTON TURNER

January 31st, 1936

THE ABYSS

SIR – All the conversations that are held by our statesmen, and all the running about from place to place, are perfectly useless – they will all come to nothing. Christ Himself has said, 'Without Me ye can do nothing.' Thus we know beforehand that they are doomed to fail. Why not try and get all the statesmen of the world to meet, and make one final attempt to get them all to lay down their arms? It must be done quickly, as at present we are heading straight for war.

M. E. WELLDON

February 10th, 1939

USELESS AIR HEADS

SIR – When is the Corporation going to provide air-raid shelters outside the main part of the town?

Walking along St. John's Road this week, I was struck by the large amount of pedestrian and vehicular traffic in this neighbourhood, and wondered where people would go if an air-raid system went off, as I could see no direction to shelters. The same applies to the St. Peter's district and the lower part of the town. I suppose our worthy(?) councillors are still on holiday and could not be called together to pass emergency local legislation, such as our national Parliament has done. I have been approached several times as to why shelters have not been made for people not in the immediate town, but whose business takes them out in the districts, but till the Council again meets I am still wondering.

BUSINESS WANDERER

September 22nd, 1939

VICE HYPOCRISY

SIR – I happened to be present at a nice little village church on the afternoon of Sunday week, and was astounded to hear the Vicar announce that the psalms would be sung, although the choir were at stoolball (this was the National Day of Prayer). I afterwards found out that this game, and tennis, were played in the neighbourhood on Sunday afternoons. Last Sunday I was told that hockey was to be played, in addition!

No wonder I have heard one or two services lately over the radio in which the preacher seemed to think that we were being punished for having the war thrust upon us, through *our* sins –

evidently not through the fault of Germany.

VISITOR

October 13th, 1939

TRIPPED MENACES

SIR – Would you grant me space in your columns to appeal to dog-owners to exercise a little care when taking out their dogs in the black-out?

Progress is difficult enough without the added hazard of outstretched dogs leads, and one is likely to be bitten by a frightened animal into the bargain.

If it is not possible for owners to exercise their dogs at any other time, they should at least provide themselves with white leads of some sort of soft material.

Most of the leads over which I have tripped during the recent dark nights have been of metal, which has resulted in severely bruised if not barked shins.

Another point: Umbrellas, especially when carried by women, are very dangerous in the black-out. It is quite easy to cause a serious eye injury through carelessness with these unwieldy articles, and they should not be carried, for the sake of other people's safety. Yours truly,

SUFFERER.

December 8th, 1939

SCREW THEM

SIR – In these times, when sleep – that precious gift

143

– is disturbed and broken, the fewer 'noises' there are the better. Therefore, may I appeal to all burgesses who keep fowls in close proximity to houses, to kill their cockerels and roosters?

Why these birds are maintained, I fail to understand, for their only function seems to be to create a raucous cycle of sound at the break of day, which continues intermittently for an hour or so afterwards. They are also consuming food which would keep another hen.

Perhaps this matter should be brought to the notice of the Minister of Home Security, for if all Fifth Columnists kept cockerels, the Fatherland would be usefully served!

H. T.

June 21st, 1940

FALSE PRETENCES HOME GUARD

SIR – We should be very glad to know whether the women now walking about the town dolled up in 'Home Guard' armlets are doing so with the authority of the War Office, or is it some sugar daddy general who is in this way giving out favour to female relatives, friends or fancy bits?

A lot of us in the Home Guard joined it because we believed that here was a man's job where there were no women, and would not be any. But evidently we are mistaken, and the Home Guard is going to be like the Army and Air Force, with a lot of women strutting about in khaki and R.A.F. uniform. Presently we shall be seeing a staid old Home Guard being directed to salute a blonde bit of goods wearing a Home Guard armlet and an officer's jacket.

If women want to do a spot of typing for the Home Guard Headquarters Staff can't they do it without wanting to dress themselves up as soldiers? When we joined the Home Guard we believed that here was a body that would be free from the effeminate touch which is tainting the administration in the Army and Air Force. It would be interesting to know whether the women of Germany are allowed to strut about in military uniform.

The seriousness of the whole thing is, however, that we of the Home Guard have lost faith in our leaders when we find they cannot do their job without being surrounded by women. If the military authorities wish to keep the Home Guard intact they must keep the women out of it, otherwise a lot of us are soon going to look for something else where there are no women.

SCRUTATOR II

October 25th, 1940

DEPRESSING LIZZIE

SIR – I had hoped that following the publication of your timely article recently on the subject of 'Screeching Lizzie' – that ghastly siren on the outskirts of Tunbridge Wells, that makes every raid warning ten times more depressing that it need be – something would have been done about it. But, as ever the official mind works very slowly, and so the piercing wails, that are almost identical for the 'alert'

145

and the 'raiders passed,' continue to exasperate the public.

The siren too, as you pointed out, is sounded usually at an appreciable time after the other warnings have ceased and, while residents have grown accustomed to the absurdity of the thing strangers in the town are still left in a state of confusion, because the wobbling strains of 'Screeching Lizzie' give the impression another 'alert' period has started.

F. M. G.

May 24th, 1941

COLD COMFORT

SIR – Last Saturday evening I had a long stroll about the town, and could not help feeling ashamed at the sight of so many hundreds of soldiers, who are awaiting the call to go to the front to fight for us, just wandering aimlessly up and down the High Street with just nothing to do but go in and out of the stuffy 'pubs' and have a drink.

I went into Calverley Park (almost deserted). There I saw an ideal bandstand (or gramophone stand), with a fine space for dancing around it, or just right for 'free and easy' communal concert. Cannot the council or some responsible people start the thing at once without forming committees? The Pantiles, too – where there is a good bandstand and space – could provide another spot, simply sighing for a 'bit of life again.'

I then went up to Calverley Park Tennis Grounds.

Four or five empty courts – but there were six soldiers there who wanted to play but could not hire rackets or balls. They were having a laugh at Royal Tunbridge Wells, and one asked me the name of this 'God d– – cemetery,' meaning 'our' park.

That piece of badly kept Common known as the Lower Cricket Ground might be used for cricket games if some sporting friends would lend the bats and balls and just advertise the fact so that the men would know.

I sincerely hope someone will make a move.

TAXPAYER

June 9th, 1944

UNHOLY STUNT

SIR – I have today had put into my door three copies of a three-page folder leaflet advertising some religious stunt at the Assembly Hall.

A more wicked waste of paper I have never seen. Why are these people allowed to waste paper in this manner when you cannot even get a copy of Shakespeare or Dickens because publishers are so rationed with paper?

I thought that it was an offence to print circulars for free distribution. If I issue a catalogue of goods I have to make the public pay for it.

JUNIUS

October 27th, 1944

The Future

Tunbridge Wells is perfect as it is. Why should it need to change, and what is wrong with the future being as perfect as the past? Can someone please explain?

CHANGE? NO THANKS

SIR – I saw your interesting report of a meeting where improvements for Tunbridge Wells were discussed. As a frequent visitor, and often meeting other outsiders who visit the town, may I venture to report what I so frequently hear, viz., 'It has a lovely Common and beautiful air, but the authorities seem bent on making it a mere suburb of London (I suppose this means Opera House, telephones, etc.), and neglect to develop the best natural features of the place.'

The spring is equal to any in Buxton, but see how 'the waters' are used there! The neighbourhood and climate are altogether better. London and suburbs are places people do not wish to be reminded of when away in the country, so why seek to 'townify' the Wells?

OUTSIDER
December 4th, 1903

SCANDALOUS PICTURES

SIR – I'm glad to see the extensive range of hoarding which indicates the beginning of the Corporation of the Mount Pleasant Improvement, and the word is deservedly spelt with a capital letter; for however much sentiment may have been expended over the half-dozen trees which are gone, I feel satisfied that the street widening once effected, every voice will acclaim its desirability, and that the newly-planted trees will in a very few years amply fill the gap now made.

We have reason to believe that the Corporation has refused to let this hoarding be used for advertising purposes – a most admirable decision, in view of the scandalous and degrading pictures which so disfigure our advertising stations, and tend to the corruption of the moral taste of our children and youth, to say nothing of our men and women.

PROGRESS

October 18th, 1901

BRAWLING WOMEN

SIR – I note that Mrs Gertrude E. Mosley prefers her own views to those held by our late Queen. This is not surprising for it is the failing of the sex.

Now, I do not think that woman's position has altered for the worse since Queen Victoria's time. If her remarks were true then, why not now? Can any additional reason be shown why women should have positions which Providence never intended they should hold?

The Almighty has given to women great powers for use in her own sphere, and those powers, if used judiciously would be far more beneficial to her than all these abstract notions she professes to want. What can be more touching than a true woman suddenly rising in mental force to be the support and comforter of her husband under misfortunes abiding with unshrinkable firmness the bitter blasts of adversity?

As the vine twined its graceful foliage about the oak, so it is beautifully ordered by Providence that woman, who is mere dependent of man in his happier hours, should be his stay and solace when smitten by sudden calamity, winding herself into the rugged recesses of his nature, tenderly supporting the dropping head and binding up the broken heart.

Will such a one be found among these street brawlers? Let true women answer.

W. CLARK

July 9th, 1909

EQUALITY OF THE SEXES

SIR – Owing to the limited time at our disposal at the very successful meeting on November 5th, of those opposed to the Suffrage movement, I had no opportunity of drawing attention to the fact that our League is now open to men, as well as to women, and that already many men have enrolled themselves as members.

May I venture to use your columns to make this generally known, and to appeal to all those men and women in accord with us to practically show their sympathy by becoming members of this league, and using any influence they possess to induce others to do the same?

The subscriptions are especially low, so as to make membership within the reach of all. From working men and women 3d. is asked, and for others from 1s. upwards.

C.W. EMSON

November 11th, 1910

BELOW THE BELT

SIR – The introduction of Manhood Suffrage lays bare the Government's scheme for preventing the enfranchisement of women. It can only be characterised as a deep insult to every woman in the country. Henceforth, should the Bill be carried, every man over 21, unless at the time of an election he happens to be the inmate of prison or a lunatic asylum, is to receive the hall-mark of citizenship, while every woman, no matter what her attainments may be, however devoted her services to the State, is to be shut out, to be branded as belonging to an inferior race....

CATHERINE WEDGWOOD
June 28th, 1912

PRATT MAT

Dear Editors, – I want to thank your for the remarkable results I have secured by using the hair formula which appeared in a recent issue of your valued paper. As directed, I went to my chemist and had him put up 3oz. Bay Rum, 1 oz Lavonna de Composée and ½ Dram Menthol Cystals. He told me that this preparation was unequalled for hair and scalp troubles, but I did not look for the astonishing benefits which followed.

For a long time I have been troubled with dandruff and falling hair, and my hair had become so thin and lifeless that I feared I would become completely bald. I applied the tonic twice a day, rubbing it into the scalp with the finger-tips, and you can imagine my delight when in the end of the third day I found that the dandruff and scalp itching had completely disappeared; within two weeks the falling out had entirely ceased, and now at the end of eight weeks the thin places are covered with a thick growth of new hair nearly six inches long. For the benefit of others who suffer as I once suffered I would suggest that you publish the formula again. Gratefully yours,

TINA H. PRATT

December 9th, 1910

[*Readers are cautioned to avoid applying where hair is not desired. – Ed*]

MOTOR SCORCHERS

SIR – Now that we are told motors have come to stay, is it not time that some Society, League or Union should be formed by those who are opposed to the excessive speeds and erratic habits of so many motorist of the present day?

Motorists have their clubs, associations, and trade conferences, which are rapidly converting the high roads to their own purposes, while the general public have no organisation on the other side.

No one fond of the country life, and in touch with country people, can view with anything but dismay the increasing invasion of the motor 'scorchers' in every part of the country.

The object therefore, of this proposed league would be to create such a body of public opinion as would influence the members of the House of Commons, who will be called upon at an early date to discuss the next Motor Car Act, and the increase of speeds which will be asked for on this opportunity.

I, for one, should be most happy to subscribe £100 to such a society, but my belief is that it would be supported by country people of all grades and positions, and that the subscriptions should be made as low as 1s and 6d.

I shall be glad to communicate with those who are disposed to agree with and support the objects I have mentioned in this letter.

JNO. HANCOCK NUNN
December 16th, 1904

TIME WASTING TRADERS

SIR – May I suggest to the tradesmen who subscribe to the Telephone Company that they would save time and trouble to their customers when answering calls by at once giving the 'name of the firm,' instead of the usual 'yes.' As a rule time is wasted by having to ask, 'Are you – ?' I know of only one tradesman in the town who always adopts this sensible plan, but there may be others.

RESIDENT
December 20th, 1907

PEDESTRIAN IGNORAMUS

SIR – Unless Mr Williams Dunnings knows something of how a motor car is driven and controlled it is useless to discuss the question with him. If he had read my letter carefully he would have seen that I stated that a motor driver varies his speed according to circumstances, and that when he does this and has his car well in hand he cannot be accused of driving to the danger of the public. A non-motorist has no idea of the ease and quickness with which a driver can regulate the speed of his car and the short space it can be pulled up in. So far as my experience has yet gone, I find that neurotic patients are benefited by motoring.

T. ELLIOT, M.D.

August 18th, 1905

TORNADO MANIACS

SIR – I have been enjoying for a week strolls about this beautiful county with a camera, getting snapshots of the varied styles of cottages along the rural roads within ten or a dozen miles of the Wells.

My object in writing is to ask you if you think the otherwise benevolently aspected motorists ever give a thought to the humble pedestrian as they pass him/her while holding to the full width of the narrow footpathless way? Fifteen feet is often the full width available. Put a big fast-moving car in the middle of this, and what is left for the humble wayfarer? It is a pitiable sight sometimes to see the poor people cringing to the side of the road to avoid the shush of whirlwind suction...

GEORGE GRAHAM

January 17th, 1913

155

FORGETFUL PEDESTRIANS

SIR – A few years ago, at any rate in the pre-war time, I remember most of the lampposts in the town were adorned with the notice, 'Keep to the right.' So few people know the ordinary rules of pedestrianism, and it is a wonder to me that more accidents do not happen…

E.A.S.

March 31st, 1916

NORTH-WARD REVOLUTION

SIR – Through the medium of your paper, will you kindly allow me to thank those who voted on my behalf at the North Ward Election?

My reason for allowing myself to be nominated as a candidate was that I feel how inadequately the working classes are represented on our Town Council. With but few exceptions, our Councillors are representatives of the professional and wealthy classes, who cannot be in touch with the workers.

W.H. COOK

October 28th, 1910

NORTH-WARD PLEASURE-MONGERERS

SIR – The North Ward contains 15 different places of worship, consisting of some highly-equipped, powerful and influential Church of England, Non-Conformists, Quakers, Plymouth Brethren and other missions, all of them professedly strong advocates of Temperance. [W]hat does last Tuesday's election reveal? That the best thing these Temperance advocates and moral reformers can do is to send representatives who are leaders of the two most demoralising businesses in existence.

I have nothing to say about these gentlemen, personally. They may be as correct in their private life as anyone else. But when we consider the interests which they represent, the inconsistency of a proportion of the burgesses, who voted on their behalf, is what strikes one. The parsons and the people will shout themselves hoarse and talk till they are red in the face at their Temperance meetings about what they intend to do with the mischievous liquor traffic. But when they want a director of their municipal life, they go to the brewer.

What do they expect the outcome of these [two] gentlemen on the Council will be? Will the brewer vote for Sunday closing or reduction of public houses, or the shortening of the hours of opening, or any of the one hundred things that temperance reformers want? Not a bit of it. Will the Opera House director vote against entertainments if they are filling the pockets of the Opera House Company?

[T]he real outcome of their being on the Council will be that they, as far as they can, will run the town in the interest of the liquor traffic and pleasure-mongering.

R.M. LANE

86, Silverdale Road,

November 4th, 1910

[*We have eliminated some of the stronger passages. — Ed.*]

AGE RAGE

SIR – In a local paper last week a letter was inserted, the purport of which was that in order to have a brighter Tunbridge Wells the depart of the ancients was much to be desired.

I am one of those ancients, as I presume over-70 will be the age limit. I am therefore interested to hear the form of ejection.

Is it a funeral pyre, as in India, which would help also to provide ashes for the cemetery paths? Are we to be driven out at the point of the bayonet, or by the bludgeon of the police by order of the Mayor?

Shall we be forewarned, and have time to gather together our bundles of treasured memories; time to let our houses, ere we go on our pilgrim way and leave our town to new generation delights? An early answer will oblige. Yours sorrowfully,

AN AGED ONE

July 4th, 1923

DISTANT VOICES

SIR – Listening-in in the early hours of Sunday morning on a 4-valve wireless receiver of my own design, I picked up the American Broadcasting Station, WGY, of the General Electric Company, New York.

He was transmitting an orchestral selection, at the close of which he stated the name and call sign of the station, and announced the names of the dances

158

to follow. The speech and music were quite clearly audible in the loud speaker.

Although American broadcasting has been received in several parts of this country, I have not heard of anyone who has received it in Tunbridge Wells, and thought, therefore, you might consider the fact of sufficient general interest to make a small mention of it.

H. FEATHERSTONE

September 14th, 1923

TV-ITIS

SIR – I notice in Tunbridge Wells the ever-growing forest of TV aerials and wonder how fast 'TV-itis' is gaining a grip on the town.

This loathsome disease if allowed to grow unchecked, will turn our youth into myopic, open-mouthed sheep, incapable of constructive thought and able only to soak up canned entertainment.

Educational value? I wonder!

OLD FASHIONED

March 3rd, 1954

DAFT DODDERER

SIR – Your correspondent, 'Old Fashioned,' is more than that – he is just plain daft!

His fear that 'TV-it is' will make youth of today the myopic morons of tomorrow is just the usual unenlightened and unimaginative point of view through the ages of people who just cannot tolerate

159

the idea of progress or see the benefits or new inventions.

They said much the same of the coming of the gramophone, the cinema and the radio, but is youth today any more myopic or incapable of constructive thought than the youth of 50 years ago?

If so, then where have our young and brilliant scientists, writers, artists and the like sprung from?

No, the fact of the matter is that 'Old Fashioned' is looking at youth with rheumy eyes and a prejudiced mind.

Myself, I neither own a TV set nor am I still on the right side of 40 – but I do realise that I am living in the second half of the Twentieth Century.

OLD YOUNG-UN

March 10th, 1954

MARTIAN NUTTERS

SIR – Like Mr Owen Lewis ('Advertiser' last week) my heart bleeds for the local Flying Saucer Club. So two schoolgirls had the temerity to 'take the mickey,' did they?

Well, well, well! I suppose they'll be the first to be sent to a lunar concentration camp when a saucerful of Martians arrive in Tunbridge Wells and take over!

I'll be convinced that flying saucers exist when one lands in the High Street – and the Martian spacemen get a very down-to-earth summons for parking in a 'no waiting' area.

DISBELIEVER

November 24th, 1954

Spiritual Stirrings

The church evidently is the pillar on which Tunbridge Wells society rests, and peace and harmony reigns more than anywhere else — or does it?

SPECIAL PLEADING

SIR – I happened to be spending last weekend in your pleasant town, and on the Sunday evening thought I would go to the Baptist Tabernacle to hear the worthy pastor of that church preach, as I am wont to do when in the neighbourhood. But on arriving at the church I found that another gentleman was taking the service.

Well, sir, all went well until the Second Prayer, when, lo!, I was astonished to hear the Reverend gentleman pray thus: –

'O God, we feel that we can ask thee tonight to relieve Ladysmith, to relieve Mafeking, to relieve Kimberley. O God, change the heart of President Kruger, remove from the hearts of President Kruger and President Steyn that animosity which has long existed there towards this England of ours.'…

Why should not the prayer have continued thus: – 'Remove those things that have created such animosity, and forgive us for not accepting our differences by arbitration, and forgive us for missing fire at Constantinople, and allowing our shells to drop into these Puritan farmers' prayer meetings. Pardon us for permitting the Jameson Raid, etc.' but no such mercy is implored for us.

E.E. LAWRENCE
January 19th, 1900

OFFENSIVE VICARS

SIR – It was with surprise that I read in last week's issue a letter signed by the Rev. Dr Townsend, coached in intemperate language attacking one of the candidates in the West Ward on the promotion of Mr Strange to the Aldermanic Bench. It appears that the sole reason Dr Townsend objects to Mr Rule is because he is a publican, the term being used by the rev. gentleman in an offensive and opprobrious manner. It is incorrect and certainly not courteous to call Mr Rule a publican. He is a licensed victualler in the true sense of the term...

I would humbly suggest to the Rev. Dr Townsend that he would be better advised endeavouring to restore harmony in the Church to which he has the honour to belong...

    J.W.

    October 13th, 1900

DESPICABLE BLOTTERS

SIR – I anticipate there will be others beside myself anxious to show in your columns their disapproval of the letter which appeared in your last issue on the above election. I will, therefore, be as brief as possible.

Dr Townsend endeavours to prove that a 'blot' will rest on West Ward should a 'publican' become one of the representatives on the Council. Well, I join issue with the Vicar there – because I find that a higher authority than the learned D.D. tells me that of two characters, the Pharisee and the Publican, it is the former not the latter whose character is despicable and a blot... may I ask the Dr Townsend which bears the cleanest record for the last forty years, St. Margaret's Vicarage or the Swan Hotel?

WEST WARD WORKING MAN

October 19th, 1900

DREARY PREACHERS

SIR – With reference to the statement in your last week's paper, by the Vicar of St. Mark's, Broadwater, I am afraid the reason he gives for the absence of the parishioners from the church is not quite the correct one. I think he will find it is the dull, dreary service at the church which keeps people away, and this applies to other churches in town, besides St. Mark's.

If the clergy will arrange to give bright, cheerful services, with sermon, not too long, and an occasional fresh preacher (not necessarily for a charity), with Hymns Ancient and Modern, instead of the poor selection they have at present, and in other ways brighten the services, they will have no cause to complain, but find their church well filled.

It is a deplorable fact at Tunbridge Wells that so many of the heads of families are either absent themselves or attend so little at the churches. Can you wonder if their son and daughter do the same?

A CHURCHMAN

May 31st, 1901

THE LENT CURE

SIR – Many of your devout readers are earnestly

anxious to keep their Lenten fast, according to the strict rules of Catholic tradition.

If, however, they do so they will probably injure their bodily health and stamina.

May I, then, advise them to take the guidance of those who have kept a perpetual Lenten abstinence from flesh food for many years, and who have learned therewith to grow even stronger, healthier, and more beautiful. Leaflets, recipes, and general hints will be gladly sent to anyone forwarding two or three stamps to 'the Provost O.G.A.,' Barcombe Hall, Paignton, South Devon.

A PHYSICAN

February 21st, 1902

NUN ATTACK

SIR – Is it not a strange thing that our countrymen seem to view with so little concern the rapid increase of Roman Catholic establishments, and the invasion of the land by a considerable number of monks and nuns? Other countries, even of the same faith, decline to receive them. France itself does not seem to take their exodus much to heart. England alone, which many years ago cleared itself of all complicity in the restless schemes of Rome, now receives these fugitives with open arms, to be in the future as 'Pricks in our eyes and thorns in our sides, and which shall vex us in the land wherein we dwell.' The experience of the past ought surely to put us on our guard against these quiet incomings of foreign religious orders, whose presence among us cannot but disturb the peace of many parishes.

VIGILANS

September 18th, 1903

DESERTED PEWS

SIR – Spending a few weeks in Tunbridge Wells, I was asked by my friend if I would accompany him to evening service at King Charles' Church, on Sunday last. Having previously heard of the historic nature of the church, and also of its attractive service, I did indeed look forward to spending a good time. Having walked about one and a half miles to the church, however, we were told we could not be admitted until the commencement of the service. When at length we were allowed in, I found, much to my surprise (after all had taken their seats), room enough for another hundred people.

I have been given to understand that the doors are closed owing to so many seats being rented, and that these seats must be keep till 6.30. That may be so, but surely better arrangements than these can be made, so as to enable those who are visitors to the church, or who cannot afford to pay for seats to enter the church at least five minutes before the service begins.

I don't know how it appeals to many people, but on Sunday last, I must confess, it reminded me of a crowd of people waiting for some theatre doors to open instead of the House of God. Really, I never thought such a thing was in existence. There are

166

many other great dangers issuing from this practice. Clergy in other parts of England say that the great problem the Church is fighting to-day is, How can we get the people to church? (especially these summer months).

I cannot say how long this has been going on, but can only say that, if continued, the time will not be long, when not only will they be glad to throw open the doors of this church, but will be glad to get in who they can.

A LOVER OF TRUE WORSHIP

June 26th, 1908

SECTARIAN BLACKMAIL

SIR – Some few days ago I was waited upon by a young man, who wanted me to give him a subscription towards a Church Building Debt. I am not connected with the sect he represented, have no sympathy with their teaching, and with this particular Church no sympathy of any kind... I write to enter my protest, as a tradesman, against this form of blackmail. If we don't give we are marked. Is there no way of stopping it?

A TRADESMAN

March 8th, 1912

A DEVIOUS GOD

SIR – It is evident that M.J.W. Lyons does not credit the theory contained in Genesis that man was made perfect, but subsequently fell from that state of perfection into sins of most diabolical order. It has always perplexed me how man came to possess this faculty of being able to disobey God's commands. Surely, when God created man, He knew what the result would be. And as man did not create his faculties – according to Genesis – God must have endowed him with them. The old plea, 'But God gave man free will,' will not strengthen the argument. God by giving man free will, knew exactly the result that would ensue. If God intended man to be perfect, it would be impossible for man to sin. May I hope that Mr Lyons will help me out of my difficulty, for I am ready and willing to believe his doctrine if he will give me reasonable and logical grounds for belief.

GABRIEL BANDERET

May 3rd, 1935

LOST IN PARADISE

SIR – In a recent report of a funeral sermon, mention was made of the Church in Paradise. Mention was also made about the Souls meeting, and holding communion with souls after death.

I should feel very grateful if some of our clergy would say in what part of the Bible we are told of the Church in Paradise and the Communion of Souls. From my own point of view, when death takes place the soul is at rest, until the Day of Judgement. Perhaps I am wrong.

ENQUIRER

February 20th, 1942

PANDERING PHARISEES

SIR – The latest pronouncements of the Archbishops of Canterbury and York, giving permission to women to attend God's house without covering their heads, is directly opposed to God's Word. See 1st Corinthians, chapter 11, verses 5 and 6.

This is simply pandering to the fashion of the day, and is utterly unworthy of the heads of the Church.

The Bible is an eternal book written for all time, and all talk about modern times and modern thought is worthless.

M. E. WELLDON

November 13th, 1942

BOUND LAGGARDS

SIR – After four years' residence I cannot help thinking, sir, that Tunbridge Wells is very much behind the times; in both Stoke Newington and Enfield, where I resided, there were splendid public libraries and reading rooms, but unfortunately a close application to business prevented my then making the use of them I should otherwise have done. Now, having retired from City life, and having plenty of opportunities of availing myself of good books, I am practically debarred from the pleasure of doing so for want of a good public library.

A.R.B.M

December 1st, 1905

Spoiled Sports

There are those who exert themselves and release excess energy and it seems that it is an endeavour that is beneficial to their health. Good luck to them, but can they keep it down please?

HIDEOUS NOISE

SIR – We have at St. John's, Tunbridge Wells, two large football fields within 200 yards of each other, in very close quarters to some of the best residential property of the parish.

I, with others, am fond of all kinds of sports in moderation, and we ask before it commences that the captain and financial workers of this company will try and modify this by making rules that no loud cheering and hideous noises be made, as we have heard in seasons gone, but show their enthusiastic spirit in the game by clapping of hands. This in the cold season would warm them, while the noises one hears would cause chill upon the lungs.

By thus passing some rules of this description it would be meeting the wishes of the inhabitants so closely within these grounds and modify the annoyance, for it is this awful yelling that is so objectionable, especially those not feeling well.

Trusting this will be taken up by the captain and financial workers in a straightforward spirit of doing unto others as they would like to be done by.

RESIDENT OF 13 YEARS

August 31st, 1906

UNMANLY LOUTS

SIR – As the matter relating to the charity cup tie, I must say I never saw a football match conducted in quite such a disgraceful manner before, and I think that the cause is not far to see when one remembers

171

the weakness of the decisions of the referee who appeared not only incompetent but at the same time afraid of his own opinions. If men are unable to control their animal feelings enough to refrain from assaulting players by deliberately kicking them, I think it is high time for such people to stop playing any manly sport.

FAIRPLAY

February 20th, 1900

BALL BIAS

SIR – I see the League committee asked the Southborough Club to censure two players, I hope they will not take any notice of the request.

Yours truly,

A. LEAGUER

P.S. – Are these cautions the outcome of jealousy at the position the Southborough team occupies in the League?

January 11th, 1901

STAUNCH DEFENCE

SIR – I was the referee on December 15th. It is interesting to note that the result of this game was 3–0 in favour of Southborough. What 'Leaguer's' grievance is I fail to understand.

It was a most unpleasant duty for me to report these players, both being personal friends. The Southborough Club and myself, also the two players reported, are as staunch friends as ever.

As to 'eyesight,' mine is wonderfully keen.

J.G. POVEY

January 15th, 1901

TIME-OUT

SIR – At the request of several members of the Committee of the Southborough Football Club, I have decided to treat the letters of 'Leaguer,' with the contempt they deserve.

W. S. MUGGRIDGE

February 15, 1901

DANGEROUS BALLS

SIR – On Sunday afternoon last I was walking with a lady round Bishop's Down, and something whizzed by her, knocking her hat and striking me on the shoulder. Turning round, I saw a golf ball in the road, and found the cause of it in some players in the Spa grounds. A couple of inches difference would have meant injury to the head or eyes of the lady or myself. No word of apology came from the golfers, and I want attention called to this locality as a dangerous one. A fence should be placed, or a notice-board, that it is unsafe to pass, unless people like to risk injury.

H.J.H

January 1st, 1904

TURF VANDALS

SIR – Two ladies on horseback galloped their horses

at a great speed across the match portion of our ground, tearing the turf fearfully and spoiling the hours of labour which have been put on the ground this year. Although our ground is not enclosed, surely anyone can see its evident use and spare us the great trouble we shall be put to to repair the damage? We should be greatly obliged to anyone who can assist us to stop this thoughtlessness on the part of those who are evidently not cricketers.

WALTER BRAND

Hon. Sec. Langton Cricket Club

March 25th, 1910

TEA-HOUSE MADNESS

SIR – Through the medium of your paper I wish to make a strong protest as a rate-payer against the erection of a tea house in St. John's Recreational Ground. In the first place, there is no general public necessity for it. The bowlers and tennis players, for whose convenience it is to be built, are all local people, who live within a stone's throw. In the second place, it is unjust and unfair to those traders who cater for tea parties. There are now less than two within a hundred yards. In the third place, it will simply end in a salaried servant being put in as manager, as I understand that although frantic overtures have been made to public caterers, no one has, as yet, had the temerity to come to terms.

JAMES MASON

April 16th, 1914

SARCASTIC HANDFULS

SIR – The enjoyment of the match between Kent and Notts at the Nevill Ground on Wednesday last week was marred by several irresponsible boys and youths sarcastically clapping Gunn and Whysall, the two first batsmen, in their fine innings of nearly 150 runs between them.

CITIZEN

July 17th, 1925

CRICKET HOOLIGANS

SIR – For several Sundays an organised cricket match has been in progress on the Lower Cricket Ground. Some twenty young fellows have been there, playing from 10 a.m. to 1 p.m. I always understood that this was not allowed; if so, where are those responsible for allowing it? If against the bye-laws, why not stopped? Why should the public be annoyed by seeing laws broken? If cricket, or any other games are allowable, one has no more to say.

A RATEPAYER

July 14th, 1939

NOT CRICKET

SIR – As long as God's day is dishonoured and cricket matches are played on that day (as they were on August 30th) there will be no better world.

M.E. WELLDON

September 11th, 1942

Shopping Hell

There is, thankfully, not much to do in Tunbridge Wells, apart from shopping. That, in itself, creates havoc enough thank you very much.

DISGRACEFUL TOYS

SIR – Can nothing be done to stop the dumping of German toys? In this town I see mechanical toys given a prominent place in a large toy bazaar plainly marked with the old familiar 'Lehmann.' This, before peace is even signed, I consider a disgrace to any town.

A VISITOR

January 19th, 1919

UNIMAGINABLE PRICES

SIR – As is my yearly custom, I am spending the autumn in this town with my husband. It is always a habit of mine whilst doing so to read the *Advertiser* each week to follow the local doings, but have not troubled to take it whilst away, which probably shows my bad taste.

In last week's paper I was more than interested in the Profiteering Act paper and discussion at the Tradesmen's Association meeting. Several utterances of Mr Murton-Neale indeed opened my eyes. Now I had a number of cases stored up in my mind of what I consider gross overcharges which I have been asked to pay in this town, and hoped to bring them before the local tribunal when they open for business. But I find if I bring these cases before the tribunal they may be classed as trivial, and I shall be liable to a fine of £50 or three months' imprisonment. Therefore, under these circumstances I shall be only too willing to let certain tradesmen go on profiteering and get my supplies from other towns,

177

or else spend the £50 on purchasing goods – thus saving the trouble of a police court case.

I also notice that a Mr T. G. Edwards made the remark that he saw things 40 to 100 per cent higher in another town recently. Surely he means 'lower.' I cannot imagine that such a town with prices, like Mr Edwards says, can be in existence.

AN ANNUAL VISITOR.

September 26th, 1919

FILTHY BREAD

SIR – Could we improve upon the way that bread is often carried about in this town.? A large basket – no cover – being slung over the shoulder of the assistant; the loaves rubbing well against his rough and, probably, often dusty coat. A white cover would do away with this unclean method. I have looked in vain for such a thing!

CLEANLINESS

October 1st, 1926

RUDE SHOPPERS

SIR – May I trespass upon your valuable space to say how, as a new-comer to this town, I have been struck by the lack of common politeness and manners shown by the so-called upper class people in this town?

For such little services as waiting while customers descend the stairs in a shop an assistant receives thanks from one person in 20. I suppose that such things as gratitude and manners are degrading to the dignity of the other nineteen.

PUBLIC SCHOOL APPRENTICE
November 4th, 1927

DEFILED MILK

SIR – We hear a lot about the steps taken for a clean milk supply. I often wonder why it is that milk bottles (especially empty ones) are placed outside street doors and garden gates and places where they can be defiled by dogs. Dogs are attentive in Tunbridge Wells, and from my own observation seem to like empty milk bottles and such-like articles.

CLEAN MILK
June 17th, 1938

POINTLESS SHOPS

SIR – Regarding the letter published last week by 'Puzzled.' My experience of shopping in the town includes a recent expedition to buy 10 shirts. I went in all the shops where I thought I might obtain them.

In one shop, two assistants were talking to one another, one was occupied serving a customer and another helping him. I managed to attract attention and made my request. The assistant, however, went back to helping the other as before. I was completely ignored and decided to leave the shop.

At another shop I was shown a leaflet where shirts might be obtained, but was not allowed to retain the leaflet to make a choice. In yet another shop, a young assistant whistled for another, and as I would require a complete range of shirts, after being cross-examined and made to feel small, away I came.

It seems that if an assistant has to get out some boxes to show you something or has to climb a pair of steps to find what the customer wants, he finds it easier to say, 'Sorry, we haven't got any.' Needless to say, I left the town and went elsewhere.

W. GOLDSMITH

January 13th, 1954

RATION ADDICTS

SIR – Have we become so steeped in the shortage mentality that we don't want this age of plenty now we've got it? I ask because I believe customers are more to blame than traders in keeping the ration spirit alive.

Several times lately I have heard people in grocer's shops ask for 'cheese on two books' and similar phrases. When will they learn to shop with freedom and ask for as much as they like of everything? Don't they want to forget ration books and Mr Strachey? Mrs Mew may have been wrong at the time she burnt her ration book – but she'd be right now, and it's time we all did the same.

HOUSEWIFE

February 24th, 1954

COLD SHOULDER

SIR – May I occupy a small space in your valuable paper to protest against the above? I should like to point out a few of the objections to the said Cold Storage, etc. It is to be open for receiving from 6 a.m. to 12 p.m. Will this mean all sorts of heavy noisy traffic up to midnight in the quiet, select neighbourhood of private and apartment houses, where many visitors come for health and rest? It will also mean ruin to some, and loss to all in Limehill and Mount Ephraim Roads, who depend on the said visitors (often invalids) for their living, besides depreciating the value of property.

I believe that Tunbridge Wells desires to keep her visitors, and this part, close to the Common, is a favourite and most convenient situation for such.

ONE WHO WOULD SUFFER

June 5th, 1912

ALL RIGHT FOR SOME

SIR – A fortnight ago I read in the *Advertiser* that during High Street repairs 'No waiting' orders in Vale Road were being rigidly enforced. True, police are always on duty at either end.

But why, whenever I drive down Vale Road, am I always held up because there is a big fruit-and-vegetable lorry unloading? Or maybe I'm just unlucky in picking the wrong time every day.

What does 'rigidly enforced' mean? Why should wholesalers' drivers and their mates be the only ones not to be put to any inconvenience by the diversion?

Who runs this town, in fact, the traders or the police?
MOTORIST
July 21st, 1954

RELUCTANT SERVICE

SIR – A favourite game of mine is to stand in certain shops in the town and watch the 'refeened' and arrogant assistants dispensing their favours with an affection or speech and manner that is pure bathos. Their 'couldn't care less' attitude is a reflection of the traders themselves, so different from the multiple stores with their London (or should I say Cockney) drive and vitality and their desire to please the customer at all costs.

If you want our custom – give us the service.
'DISGUTHTED' OF TUNBRIDGE WELLS
January 20th, 1954

Gruesome Christmas

Christmas in the typically quiet town of Tunbridge Wells should be a time of celestial bliss. In fact, it is when the gates of hell open. The silent night is ruptured by a cacophony of noise, pestilent children, not to mention the vulgar drinking that goes on. Meanwhile shoppers are put upon at every turn.

FORBIDDEN CAROLS

SIR – That was a capital leaderette in your last Friday's paper about the 'Christmas [Minstrels] Waits.' Itinerant local 'musicianers' (as they call them here) have so multiplied that suburban residents are scarcely free from them during Yuletide; and consequently they are troublesome in a variety of ways. Some of them were in the habit of advising residents of their intended visits, I have found it advisable to acknowledge the invitation, replying by sending a copy of the enclosed printed card,

> To Christmas Minstrels
> Vocal, Strings, and Brass (including the Big, Big Drum)
> In the interests of an oft damaged *lawn*, and a long suffering *garden*, I am reluctantly compelled to forbid the bands.

which has since prevented me from suffering, at this season of the year, from Christmas music and song.

ALFRED STRANGE
December 28th, 1900

DISORDERLY VOLUNTEERS

SIR – I enclose a copy of the petition sent to Major Simpson, the officer commanding the Tunbridge Wells Volunteers:

184

Being anxious for the welfare of the Volunteers under your command, we ask you to see that in the coming Christmas and New Year, when presents are rightly given to the men, all strong drink should be excluded. The stirring appeal lately put forth by Lord Roberts, entreating his countrymen to abstain from giving strong drink to the returning heroes, because by so doing they will 'lead them into excesses which must tend to degrade those whom the nation delights to humour, and to lower the soldiers of the Queen in the eyes of the world,' is one which we feel sure you will endorse as eminently reasonable.

We desire that our Volunteers in Tunbridge Wells should not be exposed to a temptation from which the Chiefs of our Army would fain deliver our soldiers soon returning from the Front. 'We lay these considerations before you in the earnest hope that you will use your powerful influence in seeking to protect our Volunteers.'

> **SPIRITED**
> January 4th, 1901

HOSING HAUNTING HOSANNAS

SIR – We, the inhabitants of the Grove Hill Road district, have for the last few nights found the old adage quite true, 'There is no rest for the wicked,' for the nuisance to which we are subject every Christmas, has this year become intolerable. Soon

185

after dark our front and back doors are pestered with bands of children 'carol singing,' who, if we do not open to them, commit nuisances. On Tuesday we had added to this a party of 'grown-ups' at it. They infested our district until 10 o'clock, and for an hour and a half we had the screeching of a horrible voice in particular. It haunts us still.

Last night, sir, we thought that the gods would be favourable, and we should have rest, but no such good fortune awaited us, for at 11 o'clock a man with a cornet commenced, and reigned supreme here for an hour and a half; between twelve and one a brass band commenced and played in all the roads round; it was nearly four o'clock before we could get pacified, and I, sir, finished up with a sleeping draught, having lost nearly three nights sleep.

This sort of thing is past endurance, and as there seems to be no law to stop it, it must be left to individual effort. As far as I am concerned, I am going to have a jolly good try to free this district. I find the water pressure on the mains in this road is 30lb. to the square inch. I shall arrange a hose direct on to this supply, and then 'Let 'em all come.'

EXHAUSTED PATIENCE

December 18th, 1903

SOUP SUCCOUR

SIR – In one fortnight, the last week of 1903 and

the first week of 1904, just when the wish of 'A Happy Christmas and New Year' was on the lips of all, a truly appalling number of crimes were committed in England, all of which were drink-caused.

If all would make a solemn promise not to offer, nor to take, intoxicants during the Christmas season it is certain that at least three-parts of the misery at Christmas time would be prevented.

It is not kind, but cruel, to put temptation in the way of those who have an especially hard time put upon them, as they minister to our wants at such a busy time. A glass of beer or spirits, if accepted from only a few of the many who offer it will result in partial intoxication, and probably in loss of employment. Again, no one can tell how drink offered at such a time may revive a craving which has apparently been conquered and subdued. We appeal to all to refuse to 'treat' others and to decline to be 'treated;' to give to messengers, porters and employees a cup of hot coffee or soup, which does not lower the temperature of the body afterwards, as spirits and beer do.

> **JOHN WARNER**
> December 15th, 1905

THE REDEEMER'S BIRTHDAY

SIR – Carlyle was out walking one day, and he wondered why he met so many drunken people. 'Oh, I know,' he exclaimed, 'It is the birthday of the Redeemer of the world! That is why these people are drunk.'

I do not suppose that there will be much drunkenness in our streets this Christmas, but what about drinking in the home, which injures health, and wastes hard-earned money just as much as does drinking in the public house? The excitement produced by strong drink is an ugly thing to witness.

There will be many soldiers and sailors home for Christmas. May I plead with your readers to refrain from tempting these fine men to drink by 'treating' them? I heard Vice-Admiral King-Hale say, with pride, that 35 per cent of our Navy are total-abstainers, and it is said that 52,000 British soldiers are pledged abstainers. But it is a sad fact that many a service man who had been true to colours the whole year through, falls before the temptation of the cruel 'treating' custom when on furlough. It is a wicked thing to tempt a man to drink. Who knows where it may end?

Last Christmas is fresh in my mind, and full of painful memories I spent it in a large garrison town. The drinking that I saw and heard of would have disgraced a pagan town in Darkest Africa! I was called upon to visit a poor widow, whose only son had just committed suicide. The wretched man had a little too much, and cut his own throat! And I had to visit the heart-broken old mother, and say – what?

E.E.H

December 21st, 1910

FASCIST TRADERS

SIR – One could hardly expect the High Street traders to keep silent at the prospect of having their road dug-up, but I do think their present attitude is high-handed and dictatorial. They have every right to protect their interests but when it comes to telling the council what to do and what not to do, they could draw the line.

If the reconstruction of the High Street is carried out it will be for the benefit of the town and townspeople in general and in the long run, High Street traders themselves will benefit in no small measure. For them to 'suggest' to the Council that work should cease for the year not later than October 16 is fantastic. Who are they to propose to the council what policy should be when the work is in the whole town interest?

Might I also suggest that, were traders to provoke the Christmas rush about the beginning of December instead of some time in October, Christmas would be less of a shopkeeper's gala.

CONSTANT SHOPPER

June 16th, 1954

CHRISTMAS BONANZA

SIR – Would some local trader care to let me know through your columns just what manufacturers are up to? Christmas has begun in the shops already; in fact, it started in October in some stores.

Do people really want to buy as early as this, or is it just the manufacturer's way of making the most of their chances and trying to foist on consumer's goods they don't really want?

It is the same with November 5 and Easter; merely because they are available in the shops as early as the end of August we have been subjected to three months of fireworks; Easter eggs, will doubtless appear in the shops as soon as the last Christmas pudding has been sold.

Are the manufacturers to blame or are we, the public at fault for letting them get away with it? Perhaps someone will be good enough to give me some answers?

PUZZLED SHOPPER

November 10th, 1954

SPINELESS TRADERS

SIR – I do not usually air my grievances by writing letters to papers, but talking to family and friends over Christmas, I have found that they shared my opinions. Would local traders care to answer the following complaint from an innocent shopper? Why, even if one shops reasonably early – say a week before Christmas – is one so frequently told:

'No, we did have some, but there's been such a run on them.' Can't they order any more? One asks.

'Oh no' is the answer in tones of resignation.

Why, if a fast-selling article is obviously helping his Christmas trade, does a trader not take active steps to get more? Why does he meekly accept the set-up of waiting till the next traveller comes round, waiting for the traveller's order to filter through the firm's offices, waiting for the despatch department to cope, waiting for the railway van to come and collect, waiting while the crate (or whatever it is) stands stacked in a goods yard waiting for a train, waiting while the train stands being unloaded at destination, waiting while the Tunbridge Wells railway van collects from the depot. Why, I ask does not the trader who wants to make money get his van (or even his private car, if the goods aren't too bulky) and drive off to the factory and demand a supply of the fast-selling article?

I only ask: I fear the answer may be that this is all a symptom of the lack of drive which traders are only too ready to denounce when they are enjoying their tirades about the slackness of 'the workers.'

PUZZLED

January 6th, 1954

REASONABLE SHOPPERS PLEASE

SIR – I feel that the letter by 'Puzzled' calls for a reply, and I would like, as a local trader, explain the situation. A manufacturer begins to plan for the following Christmas trade in January, and tries to spread the making of his goods over the 12 months. He holds showrooms in January and February where his latest samples are on view, and begins to take orders. The orders he takes largely determines the quantity of each particular line he will manufacture. I would suggest that November is 'reasonably early' to shop, and those who do so are not so likely to be disappointed.

H. WHITE

January 13th, 1954

AN ODE

We normal folk, at Christmas time
Play any stupid game;
We love to do these crazy things,
And every year the same.
Disgusted found a new delight,
But this I truly shirk.
To stand inside a busy shop
And watch the men at work.

A.F.W

January 27th, 1954